THE INCREDIBLE HULK
THIS MONSTER UNLEASHED

STAN LEE • GARY FRIEDRICH • BILL EVERETT • ROY THOMAS
ARCHIE GOOD'   TRIMPE

MARVEL *POCKET BOOK* The Incredible Hulk: This Monster Unleashed

The Incredible Hulk: This Monster Unleashed. Marvel Pocketbook Vol. 2. Contains material originally published in magazine form as Tales To Astonish #101, The Incredible Hulk (Vol. I) #102-108 & The Incredible Hulk Annual #1. First printing 2008. Published by Panini Publishing, a division of Panini UK Limited. Mike Riddell, Managing Director. Alan O'Keefe, Managing Editor. Mark Irvine, Production Manager. Marco M. Lupoi, Publishing Director Europe. Ed Hammond, Reprint Editor. Carol Bateup & Andie Leng, Designer. Office of publication: Panini House, Coach and Horses Passage, The Pantiles, Tunbridge Wells, Kent TN2 5UJ. Copyright © 1968 & 2008 Marvel Characters, Inc. All rights reserved. All characters featured in this edition and the distinctive names and likenesses thereof are trademarks of Marvel Characters, Inc. No similarity between any of the names, characters, persons and/or institutions in this edition with those of any living or dead person or institution is intended, and any such similarity which may exist is purely coincidental. This publication may not be sold, except by authorised dealers, and is sold subject to the condition that it shall not be sold or distributed with any part of its cover or markings removed, nor in a mutilated condition. This publication is produced under licence from Marvel Characters, Inc. through Panini S.p.A. Printed in Italy. ISBN: 978-1-84653-055-5

THE INCREDIBLE HULK
THIS MONSTER UNLEASHED

CONTENTS

TALES TO ASTONISH

THE INCREDIBLE

HULK

™

AND THE SUB-MARINER

MARVEL COMICS GROUP

12¢ IND. 101 MAR

APPROVED BY THE COMICS CODE AUTHORITY

WHERE WALK THE IMMORTALS!

THE INCREDIBLE HULK!

OUR TALE BEGINS AS A BONE-WEARY *BRUCE BANNER* REGAINS CONSCIOUSNESS ON A LONELY, WIND-SWEPT ISLE--

"WHERE WALK THE IMMORTALS!"

SUDDENLY, AT THE MYSTIC *COMMAND* OF A *FAR-OFF* FIGURE, HIDDEN AN UNIMAGINABLE DISTANCE AWAY, AN EERIE *CHANGE* COMES OVER THE STARTLED MAN--

--AND THE *HULK* IS BORN AGAIN!

PANORAMICALLY PRODUCED BY--
STAN LEE & MARIE SEVERIN

INKING: F. GIACOIA | LETTERING: ARTIE SIMEK

AT THAT VERY INSTANT, IN THE GOLDEN REALM OF *ASGARD*-- THE LEGENDARY LAND BEYOND THE STARS--

'TIS *DONE!* HE IS A *MONSTER* ONCE MORE!

AND *NOW,* HE SHALL SERVE THE ENDS OF *LOKI,* PRINCE OF EVIL!

HOW *FORTUNATE* THAT I NOTICED HIM UPON THAT ISLE--WHILST I WAS SEEKING THE ACCURSED *THOR!*

FOR, I HAVE FEARED REGAL *ODIN* WOULD DISCOVER THE THUNDER GOD'S *PERIL* --AND HASTEN TO *AID* HIM!

"THUS SHALL I USE MY *ENCHANTED POWER* TO TRANSPORT THE *HULK* TO ASGARD--"

"--WHERE THE RAMPAGING GIANT SHALL PROVE SUCH A *MENACE* THAT ODIN WILL HAVE NO *TIME* TO THINK OF THOR..."

AND SO --THE WONDER-MENT *BEGINS--!*

2

THEN, BEFORE THE RAGING SENTRY CAN RESUME HIS ATTACK--

WITH ONE MIGHTY *LEAP* HE DOTH CLEAR THE VERY GATES OF *ASGARD!*

BUT, SINCE *HEIMDALL* MAY NEVER LEAVE HIS ORDAINED POST--

IT SHALL BE FOR THOSE *WITHIN* TO CRUSH THE ATTACK OF YON GREEN-HUED *INVADER!*

DON'T KNOW WHERE I AM--

OR HOW I *GOT* HERE!

BUT I'LL *FIND OUT*-- WHEN I REACH THE OTHER SIDE OF THAT *WALL!*

GOOD! GOOD! ALL GOES AS *LOKI* PLANNED!

WHEN *ODIN* LEARNS OF THE MORTAL'S *INVASION*, HE SHALL *FORGET* THE PLIGHT OF HIS OWN HAPLESS *SON!*

THUS, THOR SHALL *PERISH*--AND ASGARD WILL ONE DAY BE *MINE* FOR THE TAKING!

AND, EVEN AS LOKI *GLOATS*--

THE HEART OF *ODIN* DOTH BEAT HEAVY!

MANY ARE THE *CARES* THAT DO BESET MY REGAL BREAST!

BUT, IF THE OMNIPOTENT ONE THINKS *HE* HAS TROUBLES--HOW ABOUT OUR HULKABLE HERO--?

HALT, INTRUDER!

TURN, AND GIRD THYSELF FOR FITTING *BATTLE!*

YOU THINK THE *HULK* IS SCARED OF *BATTLE??*

I CAN BEAT ANYONE WHO *LIVES!!*

THOU SHALT HAVE THY *CHANCE*-- AGAINST THE PROWESS OF-- *HOGUN!*

5

HULK HAS NO WISH FOR FURTHER *FIGHTING!*

HA! AT THE MERE *MENTION* OF VOLSTAGG'S NAME--THE FEARFUL ONE HATH *LOST* THE *WILL TO FIGHT!*

METHINKS THE MIGHTY STRANGER HATH BEEN *BEWITCHED!* THERE IS NO *EVIL* IN ONE SUCH AS *HE!*

WHO *ARE* YOU? WHERE *AM I?* WHY AM I *HERE?*

THOU KNOWEST *NOT* WHAT PLACE THIS BE?

BUT, AT THAT FATEFUL MOMENT--THE EVENT WHICH CRAFTY *LOKI* HAD DESIRED SUDDENLY COMES TO PASS--

BY THE *GOLDEN GATES!!* OUR WARRIORS ASSEMBLED NOW LEAP TO THE *ATTACK!*

THEY THINK THE GREEN-SKINNED ONE DOTH *THREATEN* THE REALM ETERNAL!

ALL--STAY THEE BACK!!

'TIS TO *NO AVAIL!* THE DIN *DROWNS OUT* THE CRY OF *FANDRAL!*

BUT, THERE BE *ANOTHER* WAY--!

9

IF THOU HEEDEST NOT MY WORDS--

THE BLADE OF FANDRAL SHALL GIVE THEE PAUSE!!

SPTANNING!

BACK--OR FACE THE WRATH OF MOUNTAINOUS VOLSTAGG!

THOUGH HIS POWER BE AKIN TO THOR HIMSELF--

HOGUN DOTH SAY HE BE NOT AN ENEMY!

AND SO SPEAKS FANDRAL!

THEY LIE!!

THEY BE IN LEAGUE WITH THE SAVAGE MONSTER!

SO SPEAKS LOKI!!

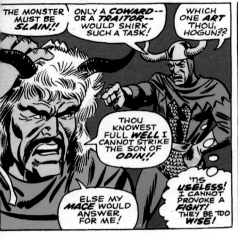

THE MONSTER MUST BE SLAIN!!

ONLY A COWARD-- OR A TRAITOR-- WOULD SHIRK SUCH A TASK!

WHICH ONE ART THOU, HOGUN??

THOU KNOWEST FULL WELL I CANNOT STRIKE THE SON OF ODIN!!

ELSE MY MACE WOULD ANSWER FOR ME!

'TIS USELESS! I CANNOT PROVOKE A FIGHT! THEY BE TOO WISE!

I WISHED FOR BATTLE--FOR ONLY THAT WOULD SERVE MY PURPOSE!

AND, IN FAILURE, THE PRINCE OF EVIL IS DEADLIEST OF ALL--!!

BUT, LOKI HATH FAILED!

10

[16]

SHARE THOU MY *SADDLE*-- FOR WE SHALL LEAP ACROSS THE *BOTTOMLESS CHASM*-- TO SEEK THE WISDOM OF *OLDAR, THE ORACLE!*

NO! HULK NEEDS *NO HORSE!*

HULK'S OWN *LEGS* CAN JUMP OVER *ANYTHING!*

THIS IS MY *CHANCE!*

THE MONSTER HAS *FAILED* ME--

THUS, THE MONSTER MUST *DIE!!*

AND, JUST AS THE SOARING TITAN REACHES THE *APOGEE* OF HIS LEAP--

A SHRILL, CACKLING *VOICE* BARKS OUT ONE SINGLE INCANTATION-- AND THE MOST INCREDIBLE *TRANSFORMATION* OF ALL TAKES PLACE ONCE MORE--

IN A STRANGE *WORLD*-- THAT I CAN'T COMPREHEND--

I'M *PLUNGING* TO CERTAIN *DOOM!*

I'VE BECOME --*BRUCE BANNER* AGAIN!!

I--I'M *FALLING*-- INTO THE YAWNING *CHASM* BELOW--

NEXT ISSUE...
THE **HULK** IN HIS **OWN MAG** AT LONG LAST!!

11

THEN, WITHIN SECONDS, THE *TRANSFORMATION* IS COMPLETED--AND *BRUCE BANNER* PLUMMETS HELPLESSLY THRU THE SEEMINGLY ENDLESS VOID!

BUT, AS DEATH RUSHES EVER NEARER THE MORTAL SCIENTIST IS *UNAWARE* OF THE COLD, CALCULATING EYES WHICH BEHOLD HIS PITIFUL PLIGHT FROM SOME ONE HUNDRED FEET *BELOW...*

ONLY HAVE *SECONDS* TO LIVE!

MY ENTIRE LIFE... FLASHING BEFORE MY EYES... *BETTY ROSS... RICK JONES,* THE ONLY ONES WHO HAD *FAITH* IN ME!

I--I'LL BE CHEATED OF THE CHANCE TO EASE THE *PAIN* I'VE CAUSED THEM... BY *DEATH!*

LOOK...ABOVE... HURTLING TOWARD US FROM ASGARD *ABOVE...'TIS...A MAN...*NOT UNLIKE A *MORTAL* IN APPEARANCE!

*TRUE...*BUT, IF HE *BE* A MORTAL, THEN HE FALLS TOWARD A FATE MOST *FITTING!*

FOR, YON CHASM LEADS BACK TO THE REALM OF HIS OWN KIND... *EARTH!*

BESIDES, WHAT TIME HAVE THE *EXECUTIONER* AND THE *ENCHANTRESS* FOR SUCH PETTY MATTERS... WHEN THE *REALM ETERNAL* SOON WILL BE OURS FOR THE *TAKING?*

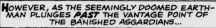

HOWEVER, AS THE SEEMINGLY DOOMED EARTH-MAN PLUNGES *PAST* THE VANTAGE POINT OF THE BANISHED ASGARDIANS...

BUT, THE MORTAL MAY HAVE TIDINGS OF *HERCULES*... HE TO WHOM I HAVE GIVEN MINE *HEART*!

HE MUST BE *SPARED*!

I SAY THEE *NAY*... LEST THE LONGINGS OF THY FEMALE HEART INTERFERE WITH FAR MORE *IMPORTANT* PROCEEDINGS!

BUT, BEFORE HER PARTNER IN EVIL CAN *ACT*, A SINGLE GESTURE FROM THE BEAUTEOUS MISTRESS OF ENCHANTMENT SENDS A BOLT OF PURE, MYSTIC *ENERGY* HURTLING THROUGH THE VOID, UNTIL...

SOME STRANGE FORCE... SLOWING MY *DESCENT*... SUSPENDING ME IN *MID-AIR*!

PERHAPS... ALL IS NOT *LOST*! THERE STILL MAY BE... *HOPE*!

AND INDEED, SECONDS *LATER*...

THE MORTAL IS *SAVED*! NOW I MUST BRING HIM *TO* ME!

FIE! BEFORE THIS DAY IS DONE, YOU SHALL *REGRET* THIS ACTION... FOR SUCH A DELAY CAN ONLY *HINDER* OUR SCHEDULE FOR THE INVASION OF *ASGARD*!

I'M BEING *LIFTED* ... BY SOME STRANGE FORCE WHICH SEEMS TO COME FROM THAT *WOMAN* ON THE LEDGE ABOVE ME!

THEN, AS THE STARTLED SCIENTIST IS LIFTED TO SAFETY, THE EYES OF THREE *ASGARDIANS* PEER INTO THE BLACK EMPTINESS OF THE CHASM INTO WHICH HE FELL FROM HIGH ABOVE...

I FEAR THE GREEN-HUED STRANGER HATH MET HIS *DEATH* BY NOW! FOR HE FADED FROM SIGHT LONG *MINUTES* AGO!

YAY, VOLSTAGG! FOR ONCE WE BE IN *AGREEMENT*! TRULY NO MAN, EVEN IF HE BE *IMMORTAL*, COULD SURVIVE SUCH A *PLUNGE*!

THEN ALL THAT BE LEFT IS FOR US TO *CONTINUE* OUR JOURNEY TO CONSULT *OLDAR*! PERHAPS *SHE* HATH THE POWER TO ENLIGHTEN US AS TO FROM WHENCE THE STRANGER *CAME*... AND FROM WHENCE HE RECEIVED SUCH *STRENGTH*... AND *VALOR*!

3

THUS, AFTER AN HOUR'S RIDE, THE THREE IMMORTALS FIND THEMSELVES AT THE EDGE OF A DARK, MYSTERIOUS *FOREST*...

NO! AHEAD LOOMS THE FORBIDDEN FOREST... AND THE ENCHANTED *GONG!* TO STRIKE ITS SURFACE IS TO SUMMON *OLDAR, THE ORACLE!*

AND SURELY NONE BE MORE SUITED TO PERFORM THAT DEED THAN *VOLSTAGG!* WHAT *SAY* THEE, VALOROUS ONE?

I? SURELY HOGUN DOTH *JEST!* THE FIGHTING COURAGE OF VOLSTAGG NEED NOT BE WASTED ON SUCH TRIVIAL CHORES!

BE IT THE DEED'S LACK OF *IMPORTANCE* ...OR THE EERIE *SURROUNDINGS* WHICH MAKE THEE SHY AWAY?

THOU DOST SPEAK THE WORDS OF A *COWARD,* HOGUN! BUT, IF *THOU* BE AFRAID TO PERFORM SAID TASK, THEN VOLSTAGG *WELCOMES* THE CHALLENGE!

THERE BE LITTLE TO FEAR IN PLAYING BUT A *MUSICAL INSTRUMENT* FOR ONE WHO HATH FACED *DEATH* THOUSANDS OF TIMES... *BE* THERE?

KNOW YOU, HOWEVER-- BUT FOR THE COURAGE OF *VOLSTAGG,* THOU WOULDST REMAIN FOREVER *IGNORANT* OF THE DEPARTED STRANGER!

NO! WHAT TRICKERY IS *THIS?*

THE VIBRATIONS DO HURL ME *BACK*...AS THOUGH I WERE BUT A LEAF IN A *GALE!*

BONG

THEN, AS THE AMAZED ASGARDIAN WARRIORS LOOK ON IN AWE-STRICKEN SILENCE, A GHASTLY *APPARITION* TAKES SHAPE OUT OF THE VIBRATING AIR WAVES WHERE ONCE THE *GONG* STOOD...

STAND YE *STILL,* MY STEED! IN YON CLEARING...*THE ORACLE COMES!*

HOLD BACK, YE COME FROM LAND AFAR, YE STAND IN THE PRESENCE OF... *OLDAR!*

LOOK! 'TIS SOME...SOME FEARSOME *GHOSTLY IMAGE!* LET US *FLEE*...LEST IT BE SOME ALL-CONSUMING FORCE OF *EVIL!*

4

STAND FIRM, YE HAVE NO NEED TO FEAR-- 'TWAS YOU WHO SUMMONED OLDAR HERE!

DRAW NEAR AND STATE WHAT YE MUST KNOW, ERE YOUR TIME BE GONE--AND I MUST GO!

BEWARE, MY FRIENDS! VOLSTAGG WILL SPARE YOU FROM THE EVIL SPELLS OF YON FRIGHTFUL WITCH!

STAND THEE BACK, VOLSTAGG! THIS IS OLDAR, SHE OF WHOM WE HATH COME IN SEARCH!

BUT NOW YOUR SEARCH HATH ENDED HERE, LAY DOWN YOUR ARMS AND COME YOU NEAR!

TRUST HER NOT, MINE GULLIBLE COMPANIONS! YON FIENDISH APPARITION BE EVIL PERSONIFIED! HER ONLY WISH IS TO SLAY US!

STILL THY TONGUE, COWARDLY ONE! OUR ONLY PURPOSE BE TO HEAR OLDAR... AND HEAR HER WE SHALL!

THEN SILENT BE THEE WHILE I ENHANCE, THE SPIRITS OF MY ALL-KNOWING TRANCE!

THROUGH ENDLESS TIME AND VOIDLESS SPACE, LET MY MYSTIC MIGHT ALL BARRIERS ERASE! THAT OLDAR NOW MAY LET BE KNOWN, THE POWERS VESTED IN HER ALONE!

NEVER HAVE MINE EYES BEHELD SUCH MAGIC! IN BUT THE TWINKLING OF AN EYE HER AGE HATH BEEN REDUCED BY COUNTLESS YEARS!

THAT IS BUT A TRACE OF OLDAR'S POWERS! THOU SHALT SEE MORE IN THE COMING HOURS! BUT YE CAME TO LEARN OF IMPENDING DANGER-- WHICH LOOMS FOR ASGARD DUE TO A STRANGER!

FOR THE LAST TIME, BANNER--STOP THIS INSANE PROJECT! IT'S TOO DANGEROUS!

NO, IGOR! WE'RE TOO CLOSE TO SUCCESS...TOO CLOSE TO GIVING OUR COUNTRY A WEAPON SO POWERFUL IT CAN ASSURE WORLD PEACE FOREVER!

HE CAME TO ASGARD FROM EARTH BELOW-- NOW, OF HIM YOU SHALL LEARN ALL I KNOW!

5

[23]

"THEN AS THE SCIENTIST DID WAIT, THE TEST WHICH COULD DECIDE EARTH'S *FATE*, THE *G-BOMB* SAT IN WAITFUL SILENCE, FOR A *FINGER* TO TOUCH OFF ITS TERRIBLE *VIOLENCE!*"

IN JUST A FEW MORE *SECONDS*, WE'LL KNOW WHAT HAPPENS WHEN THE *GAMMA RAYS* ARE RELEASED IN THE MOST POWERFUL EXPLOSION MAN HAS EVER *KNOWN!*

WAIT! GOOD LORD, THERE'S A BOY DRIVING THROUGH THE *TEST AREA!* HE'LL BE *KILLED!*

...UNLESS I CAN GET OUT THERE AND *WARN* HIM...BEFORE IT'S *TOO LATE!*

IGOR! DELAY THE COUNT DOWN UNTIL I CAN GET THAT KID TO *SAFETY* ...AND DON'T WASTE A *SECOND!*

CERTAINLY, DR. BANNER! WHATEVER YOU *SAY!*

I'VE WORKED IN BANNER'S SHADOW *LONG ENOUGH!* THIS IS MY CHANCE TO TAKE *OVER!*

IF I DON'T ISSUE THE ORDER, IT'LL BE BYE-BYE *BANNER!*

"THEN, IGNORING ALL IMPENDING DANGER,... BRUCE BANNER RISKED ALL TO SAVE A *STRANGER!*"

KID... GET OUTTA HERE! YOU'RE IN A FORBIDDEN *TEST AREA!*

COOL IT, DADDY! IT AIN'T LIKE THEY WERE BLOWIN' THE *BIG ONE* OR SOMETHIN'!

GUESS AGAIN, BOY! A TEST BOMB'S SET TO GO OFF ANY *SECOND! COME ON!*

DON'T HAND ME THAT JIVE, MAN! I GOTTA... *BOMB? ANY SECOND?*

"AS HE CALLED BANNER DASHED FOR COVER, THE FATEFUL FINGER OF *ANOTHER,* REACHED OUT AND TOUCHED THE BUTTON DREAD, WHICH PAINTED BANNER'S FUTURE...*DEAD!*"

THERE! YOU'RE SAFELY IN THE *SHELTER* AND... *AAGGGHHHH!*

6

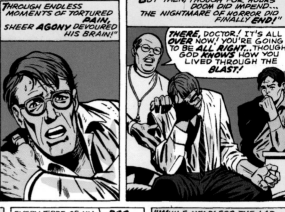

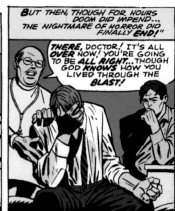

"BUT, LO THERE **WAS** NO EASY WAY FOR SUCH AS HE MEN TO IMPOUND, AND SO HE STALKED LIKE BEAST AT BAY FOR MEN TO HUNT, AND HATE AND **HOUND!**"

NO MATTER HOW HARD THEY **TRY**... THEY'LL **NEVER** KILL HULK!

EVERYONE **FEARS** HULK! BUT... NO ONE **UNDER-STANDS!** HULK MUST ALWAYS BE... **ALONE!**

NO PLACE FOR HULK TO **HIDE!** EVERYWHERE MEN **KNOW** HIM... **CHASE** HIM... GIVE HIM NO **PEACE!**

SO HULK HAVE NO CHOICE BUT TO **MAKE** HIS PEACE... WITH HIS **STRENGTH!**

MUST BE DESTROY

AIR FORCE BASE IN SHAMBLES-H HULK ESCAPE

HULK CA PANIC IN FEAR GR

LEADERS UNITE IN WAR

COAST TO COAST SEARCH IS ON HULK B

PRESIDENT ORDERS HULK

WORLD PRESS

HULK DESTROYS NAVAL FORCES JOIN IN B

"AND SO IT WAS WHAT MAN HAD WROUGHT, HE SOUGHT TO PUT ASUNDER! HIS GREATEST HEROES **FOUGHT** THE HULK, LIKE **THOR**, THE GOD OF THUNDER!"

"UNTIL HIS MIND GREW **CLOUDED**, AND HE KNEW NOT RIGHT FROM **WRONG**, THE TOTAL DESTRUCTION OF ALL **MANKIND** BECAME HIS BATTLE SONG!"

ALL MEN HATE HULK-- AND HULK HATE ALL **MEN!** HULK CAN'T HAVE **REST** TILL THEY ALL **DIE!**

"THE **EXECUTIONER**, SILVER SURFER, SUB-MARINER, AND MANY MORE, COULD NOT HALT HIS VENGEFUL WRATH-- AND NOW HE THREATENS **ASGARD'S DOOR!**"

TELL US **MORE**, O ALL-KNOWING ORACLE! YOU SPEAK AS THOUGH THE GREEN-SKINNED BEHEMOTH YET **LIVES**-- AND MAY **ATTACK** FAIR ASGARD!

THAT BE FOR **THEE** TO SORT OUT-- BEFORE THIS DAY IS O'ER, FOR OF **THIS** PRECIOUS TIME, I FEAR YOU HAVE NO **MORE!**

9

SHE **AGES**--FADES FROM OUR VERY **SIGHT**...LIKE SOME ENCHANTED **WRAITH!**

AYE...AND WITHOUT TELLING US THAT WHICH WE MOST DESPERATELY SOUGHT TO **LEARN**...

...WHETHER THE **GROTESQUE** STRANGER STILL **LIVES!** AND, IF HE DOES...DOES HE **INDEED** THREATEN THE **REALM ETERNAL!**

AND, AS THE ASGARDIANS **PONDER** THAT BURNING QUESTIONS, LITTLE DO THEY REALIZE THAT, AT THAT VERY MOMENT, THE **ANSWER** IS BEING FORMULATED THOUSANDS OF FEET **BELOW** THEM...

SPEAK, MORTAL--'ERE MY PATIENCE GROWS **THIN!** TELL ME WHAT YOU KNOW OF THE AVENGER CALLED **HERCULES!**

I--I DON'T **KNOW** ANY HERCULES! THERE ARE **MILLIONS** OF MEN ON EARTH--I DON'T KNOW THEM **ALL!**

HAVE YOU NOT HEARD **ENOUGH?** CAN YOU NOT **SEE** THE MORTAL HAS NOT THE INFORMATION YOU SEEK?

YOU ARE **RIGHT!** SLAY **HIM!** HE SERVES US NO **PURPOSE!**

I SHALL DO **EXACTLY** THAT! NOW, MORTAL-- PREPARE TO TASTE THE DEATH BLOW OF...**THE EXECUTIONER!**

IT--IT'S ALL SO **UNREAL!** THESE STRANGE PEOPLE... WITH THEIR ARCHAIC **SPEECH PATTERNS!**

THEY SAVE MY **LIFE**... THEN ASK ME ABOUT THE EXISTENCE OF A CHARACTER FROM ANCIENT **GREEK** MYTHOLOGY...AS IF I SHOULD **KNOW** HIM!

THEN, BECAUSE I CAN'T **ANSWER**...THEY'RE GOING TO **SLAY** ME! WHAT SORT OF MADNESS **IS** THIS? AM I TO DIE WITHOUT **LEARNING?**

SUDDENLY, ALMOST AS IF IN **ANSWER** TO BRUCE BANNER'S **QUESTION**...

WHAT BASE TRICKERY IS **THIS?**

HAVE MY EYES **FAILED** ME? AM I GOING **MAD?**

10.

THEN, AS THE TWO EVIL IMMORTALS LOOK ON IN *DIS-BELIEF,* THE MOST AMAZING TRANSFORMATION IN *MARVELDOM** ONCE AGAIN TAKES PLACE...

*OR IN ANY *OTHER* DOM FOR THAT MATTER. --SET-IT-STRAIGHT STAN.

IT--IT'S HAPPENING *AGAIN!* NO WAY...TO *STOP* IT!

BODY... *STRAINING!* EVERY MUSCLE... *THROBBING...* I'M ONCE MORE BECOMING...

THE HULK!

BEHOLD!

BEFORE MY VERY EYES THE EARTH-MAN HATH TURNED INTO THE *GREEN-SKINNED BEHEMOUTH...*

--WITH WHOM I DID DO BATTLE ONCE *BEFORE!**

*WAY BACK IN *ASTONISH #77,* REMEMBER? --SURE-FIRE STAN.

STAND THEE *BACK,* EXECUTIONER--WHILST THE SPELLS OF THE *ENCHANTRESS* HALT THE THREAT OF YON THREATENING CREATURE!

BY THE *GOLDEN GATES* OF ASGARD --LET THE MONSTER BE...

NAY!

WHEN LAST I MET THIS LOATHSOME GARGOYLE, I TASTED THE BITTER WINE OF *DEFEAT!*

BUT *NOW,* MINE ENCHANTED AXE SHALL SHOW THE BEAST NO *QUARTER!*

IT BE ONLY *FITTING* THAT HE DIE BY MY *BLADE!*

YOU HELD THE WEAK-LING *BANNER*--BUT NO MAN CAN KEEP *HULK* PRISONER!

WHUMP!

11

NAH! I WAS TOO *FAST*-- DODGED YOUR PUNY AXE!

NOW *YOU* FEEL THE STRENGTH OF THE *HULK!*

UUNNNNHH!

AN AWESOME DISPLAY OF BRUTE *STRENGTH*...

BUT THAT IS LITTLE *MATCH* FOR THE MYSTIC POWERS OF MY *AXE*...AS YOU SHALL SOON *SEE!*

STRANGE FORCE... *GRIPPING* HULK!

HO! HOW EASILY YOU CRUMBLE... AS ASGARD *ITSELF* SHALL SOON FALL TO ME!

STRENGTH... *FADING!* MUST ACT... *QUICKLY!* BEFORE IT'S... *TOO LATE!*

SEE HOW YON GIANT *FALTERS,* MY BEAUTEOUS ACCOMPLICE? AND, WITH THE *TROLL LEGIONS* AT OUR SIDES, SO SHALL *ASGARD* CRUMBLE BEFORE US!

BUT, AT THAT PRECISE *INSTANT*...

WHA...?

NO ONE CAN DEFEAT HULK!

THE CREATURE STRUCK THE GROUND WITH SUCH *FORCE* THAT THINE AXE WAS JARRED FROM THY *HANDS!*

NOW WE SHALL PLAY THE GAME *MY* WAY!

LET THE *TROLL LEGIONS* ATTACK!

KCHOOM

12

AND NOW, MINIONS OF THE TROLL KINGDOM, FOLLOW *ME*...TO THE ULTIMATE GLORY IN WHICH WE SOON SHALL *REVEL*...

...THE TOTAL DEFEAT OF ASGARD!

NOW YOU SPEAK AS YOU TRULY *ARE*...A RULER BORN...A MAN DESTINED TO *CONQUER!* GIVE THE *WORD*...AND THE ENCHANTRESS SHALL FOLLOW THY PATH TO *GLORY!*

BUT, AS THE INVASION FORCE BEGINS ITS MARCH TOWARD THE UNSUSPECTING SURFACE REALM OF *ODIN*...

SOON ASGARD FACES INVASION-- AS IT HAS NOT SEEN IN *PAST*, AND OF THE MORTAL MEN CALL *HULK*-- THEE HAVE NOT SEEN THE *LAST!*

BUT, WHO WOULD *DARE* TO...

IT IS *NO USE!* SHE HATH FADED FROM OUR *SIGHT!*

AND THE PROPHECIES SHE HATH *MADE* TO US LEAVE US WITH BUT ONE COURSE OF *ACTION!*

ON TO ASGARD!

THEN, AS THE WARRIORS THREE BEGIN A DESPERATE DASH TO *WARN* THE CITY, THE GLEAMING SPIRES OF ASGARD GLIMMER QUIETLY IN THE PEACEFUL GLOW OF A GLISTENING SUN...

WHILE, THOUSANDS OF FEET *BELOW*, A MORE PERPLEXED THAN EVER *HULK* DECIDES UPON A COURSE OF *ACTION*...

HULK CAN'T FIND WAY *OUT*-- MUST GO BACK THE WAY HE *CAME!*

AND, IF ENEMIES STILL *WAIT* FOR ME--HULK WILL *SMASH* THEM!

14

BUT, AFTER BATTERING HIS WAY THROUGH THE WALL HE HAD BROUGHT DOWN ONLY MOMENTS *BEFORE*, THE HULK FINDS...

GONE! ENEMIES WERE *AFRAID* OF HULK... KNEW THERE WAS NO WAY TO *DEFEAT* HIM!

MUST HAVE RUN AWAY IN... *WAIT... ABOVE!* SAME MEN WHO ATTACKED HULK ARE CRAWLING TOWARD *SKY!*

MAYBE THEY'LL LEAD HULK BACK TO *SURFACE...* WITHOUT *KNOWING* IT!

NO WAY OUT *BELOW* ME-- ONLY *DARKNESS!*

HULK HAVE NO *CHOICE...* MUST FOLLOW ENEMY *UPWARDS!*

MUST JUMP AS HIGH AS I CAN... *NOW!*

HOWEVER, EVEN THE ALL-POWERFUL MUSCLES OF THE *HULK* ARE NOT ENOUGH TO PROPEL HIM THE SEVERAL THOUSAND FEET TO THE CHASM'S *MOUTH!*

HULK *MISSED* ...COULDN'T JUMP *HIGH* ENOUGH!

ROCKY WALLS *SLIPPERY...* HARD TO HANG *ONTO!*

HULK STARTING TO...

...*FALL!*

AS THE GREAT, GREEN GARGANTUA AGAIN PLUNGES TOWARD SEEMING *DEATH*, HOWEVER, HIS HUGE HAND REACHES OUT IN A FINAL, DESPERATE ATTEMPT TO GRAB A PROTRUDING *LEDGE...*

MADE IT!

NOW... IF ONLY... I CAN PULL MY WAY... *UP!* ONLY *CHANCE!* MUST... CLAW WAY... TO *TOP!*

15

WHILE, AT THAT VERY MOMENT, AT THE MOUTH OF THE YAWNING CHASM, THE TROLL ARMIES POUR FORTH LIKE AN ENDLESS STREAM OF VENOM FROM A STRIKING *COBRA*--LASHING OUT TOWARD THE VERY HEART OF *ASGARD*...

ONWARD! ASGARD MUST BE OURS!!!

AND, IN THE IMPERIAL THRONE ROOM OF THE OMNIPOTENT *ODIN*...

AND OLDAR *ALSO* WARNED THAT ASGARD WOULD BE ATTACKED...

THE INVADERS *COME!* EVEN NOW I SEE THE CLOUD RAISED BY THEIR ARMIES ON YON DISTANT *HORIZON!*

SO BE IT! ASGARD HATH FACED INVASION BEFORE--AND *HELD!* SO SHALL SHE DO IT *AGAIN!* SOUND THE CALL TO *ARMS!*

TO ARMS! TO ARMS! THE REALM ETERNAL STANDS IN DANGER!

THE *BATTLE CALL!* WHO DARES TO TRED ON THE SACRED SOIL OF ASGARD?

'TIS NOT FOR US TO *QUESTION* THE WILL OF ODIN! WE CAN ONLY OBEY HIS IMPERIAL *CALL!*

THEN, AS THE MIGHTY ARMIES OF ASGARD BRACE FOR THE COMING *BATTLE...*

ALL IS IN *READINESS!* WITH THE AID OF MY ENCHANTING MIGHT--THE MEN OF ASGARD WILL STAND *HELPLESS* BEFORE THE TROLL *HORDES!*

THUS, LET THE ONSLAUGHT *BEGIN!*

AND SURELY, BEFORE THE SUN SETS, ASGARD SHALL BELONG TO... THE *ENCHANTRESS* ...AND THE *EXECUTIONER!*

HOWEVER, AS THE FIRST CLASHES OF COMBAT RESOUND THROUGHOUT THE *REALM ETERNAL...*

THE *TOP!* HULK HAS *ESCAPED!* HULK IS *FREE!*

BUT, WHAT'S THE *NOISE* I HEAR...IN THE *DISTANCE?*

SOUNDS LIKE *FIGHTING!* MAYBE MEN WHO TRIED TO HELP HULK--IN *TROUBLE!* HULK MUST GO *SEE!*

16

AND, IN TROUBLE *ARE* THE THREE ASGARDIANS WHOSE GOAL IT WAS TO AID THE HULK--ALONG WITH THE *REST* OF THEIR PEOPLE...

I--I CANNOT RAISE MINE SWORD TO *SMITE* THE ENEMY!

NOR CAN *I!* METHINKS THE LEGIONS OF ASGARD ARE *BEWITCHED!*

SLAY THEM! SLAY THEM!

ASGARD MUST BE DESTROYED --TO THE *LAST* MAN!

BUT, THE FUTURE OF THE REALM ETERNAL IS NOT SO BLEAK AS IT *SEEMS!* FOR, AT THAT SAME MOMENT, A FEW HUNDRED YARDS *AWAY...*

HULK WAS *RIGHT!* ENEMIES FROM BELOW *ATTACK* HIS FRIENDS!

BUT UNDER-EARTH CREATURES CAN'T *WIN*-- NOT WHEN *HULK* TURNS ON THEM!

THEN, AS A PAIR OF STEEL-STRONG LEG MUSCLES PROPEL THEIR OWNER THROUGH THE ASGARDIAN *SKIES...*

LOOK... UP ABOVE US!

IT IS THE GREEN-SKINNED BEING WHO FOUGHT US *BELOW!*

KILL HIM! THIS TIME HE CANNOT *ESCAPE* US!

THEY'RE ALL *FOOLS!* HULK BEAT THEM *ONCE*--BUT THEY ATTACK HIM *AGAIN!*

THERE'RE *THOUSANDS* OF THEM--ALL WITH *WEAPONS!* BUT THEY STILL NO MATCH FOR THE *HULK!*

SUDDENLY, BEFORE THE TROLLS CAN REACH HIM, THE HULK CLUTCHES HIS GIGANTIC FISTS TOGETHER--RAISES THEM HIGH ABOVE HIS *HEAD,* AND...

HULK CAN BEAT A *HUNDRED...* A *THOUSAND* MEN! HULK ONLY NEED HIS *STRENGTH!*

NOW HULK'S ENEMIES *LEARN...* IF THEY *LIVE!*

WHAT IS THIS?

THE VERY EARTH *BELOW* US SEEMS TO *TREMBLE*--AND CAUSES US TO LOSE OUR *BALANCE!*

IT IS THE GREEN-SKINNED *MORTAL* WHO HAS DONE THIS! BUT I CAN-NOT BE *DEFEATED* ...NOT WHEN VICTORY IS SO *NEAR!*

FLEE! THE GROUND *ITSELF* HAS TURNED AGAINST US!

THHOOM!

BUT, WHILE THE TROLLS RUN FOR THEIR VERY *LIVES*...

FIE!

WITH WHAT MANNER OF COWARDS HAVE WE *ALLIED* OUR-SELVES?

HOWEVER, IT SEEMS A CERTAIN GREEN-SKINNED *GIANT* JUST MIGHT HAVE *OTHER* IDEAS! FOR, AT THAT PRECISE INSTANT...

ENEMIES RUN-- BUT THEY CAN'T GET *AWAY!* I'LL JUMP INTO *CRACK* THAT I FORCED OPEN--

...AND SPREAD IT UNTIL GROUND SPLITS LIKE IN BIG *EARTH-QUAKE!*

THE JACKALS FLEE IN ABJECT *TERROR* AT A SLIGHT TREMOR OF THE *SOIL!*

BUT IT MATTERS *NOT!* VICTORY *STILL* WILL BE OURS!

AND, AS THE HULK STRAINS HIS EVERY MUSCLE TO THE HILT TO *ACHIEVE* HIS GOAL...

THEN, WITHIN THE TINIEST FRACTION OF A *SECOND*, AN UNSEEN BOLT OF FORCE RIPS INTO THE GROUND TROD BY THE FLEEING TROLLS, AND...

--*AAAIIIEEEE!*-- THE GROUND *OPENS!* IT IS *ENGULFING* US!

I KNOW NOT WHO THIS MIGHTY ALLY *BE*--BUT HIS EFFORTS SHALL NOT GO *UNAIDED!*

BY THE SUPREME POWER VESTED IN THE *SCEPTOR OF STRENGTH*, LET THE HUNGRY EARTH OPEN ITS *JAWS*-- AND *SWALLOW UP* THOSE WHO WOULD DESECRATE MY *REALM!*

WHILE, ON THE *OTHER SIDE* OF THE NEWLY OPENED PIT...

GROUND TEARING *IN TWO*--JUST AS HULK *KNEW* IT WOULD!

HULK WILL COVER HOLE WITH *ROCKS!* ENEMIES MUST NEVER COME TO *SURFACE* AGAIN!

CAN'T STOP *NOW*, THOUGH-- NOT UNTIL ALL GO BACK *UNDERGROUND*... WHERE THEY *COME* FROM!

UNDERGROUND MEN MUST NEVER *FORGET* HULK! THEY MUST REMEMBER NO ONE CAN *BEAT* HIM!

18

BUT, WHILE THE HULK PUTS FINISHING TOUCHES ON THE TASK AT **HAND...**

THOSE SNIVELING **COWARDS!** I SHOULD NEVER HAVE LET THE EXECUTIONER CONVINCE ME TO LET THEM **JOIN** US!

NOW OUR CAUSE IS TRULY **LOST**--FOR MY SPELLS HAVE NO **EFFECT** ON THE ACCURSED **ODIN!**

STILL, HAD IT NOT BEEN FOR THE ABOMINABLE **MORTAL,** WE MIGHT HAVE **WON** THE BATTLE--BEFORE ODIN REALIZED WHAT WAS **HAPPENING!**

THUS, EVEN IN **DEFEAT,** SHALL THE ENCHANTRESS HAVE HER FINAL **REVENGE** ...THE DEATH OF THE MORTAL MEN CALL **HULK!**

SUDDENLY, AS THE HULK TURNS TO FACE AN ONRUSHING **FANDRALL...**

ZAP!

NO! OUR MYSTERIOUS ALLY FROM EARTH IS **STRUCK DOWN** AS I APPROACH HIM!

COULD FATE BE SO CRUEL AS TO REWARD HIS NOBLE DEEDS IN THE BEHALF OF ASGARD WITH... **DEATH?**

HE--HE BREATHES **NOT!** TRULY HE BE...

NAY, BRAVE FANDRALL-- FOR NONE WHO HATH LIFTED HIS HAND IN BEHALF OF **ODIN** MAY SUFFER SUCH A FATE!

BY ALL THE POWER WHICH BE MINE TO COMMAND...THE MORTAL SHALL **LIVE!**

SO BE IT!

AND, INDEED, EVEN BEFORE THE SCEPTOR IN ODIN'S HAND CAN BE **LOWERED...**

WHO--WHO ARE **YOU?** WHY AM I **HERE?**

WHY DO YOU POINT **WEAPON** AT HULK?

HULK WAS **WRONG!** YOU'RE NOT MY FRIENDS **EITHER!** NO ONE IS HULK'S FRIEND!

STAND BACK, MORTAL-- LEST YOU FEEL THE WRATH OF **ODIN!**

YOU CAN'T THREATEN *HULK!* HULK WILL *DESTROY* YOU-- JUST LIKE HE DID THOSE THAT *ATTACKED* YOU!

INSOLENT FOOL! NONE MAY ADDRESS THE OMNIPOTENT PRESENCE IN SUCH A *TONE!*

MY LORD...WAIT! I BEG OF THEE TO HAVE *MERCY!*

THE EARTHLING KNOWS NOT WHAT HE *SAYS*--FOR HIS BRAIN HATH BEEN AFFECTED BY SOME MYSTERIOUS *RAY!*

WHAT? BALDER DARES TO INTERFERE WITH THE JUSTICE OF *ODIN?*

NAY, MY LORD! HE BEGS THEE TO REALIZE THAT THE MORTAL IS NOT *RESPONSIBLE* FOR HIS DEEDS!

FANDRAL SPEAKS THE *TRUTH,* OMNIPOTENT ONE! ALL THIS HATH BEEN MADE KNOWN TO US BY *OLDAR, THE ORACLE!*

ENOUGH! THE DECISION OF ODIN HATH ALREADY BEEN *RENDERED!*

SINCE THE MORTAL DID STRIKE A HAND FOR ASGARD IN *BATTLE...*HIS PENALTY SHALL NOT BE *DEATH!*

INSTEAD, HE SHALL BE RETURNED FROM WHENCE HE DID *COME*--FOR SUCH AS *HE* CAN HAVE NO PLACE WITHIN THE REALM ETERNAL!

I HAVE SPOKEN!

EVERYTHING... GOING *BLANK!* MOVING...SO *FAST...* BUT...TO *WHERE?*

AS IF YOU HADN'T ALREADY GUESSED--

TO BE

HULK-INUED!

20

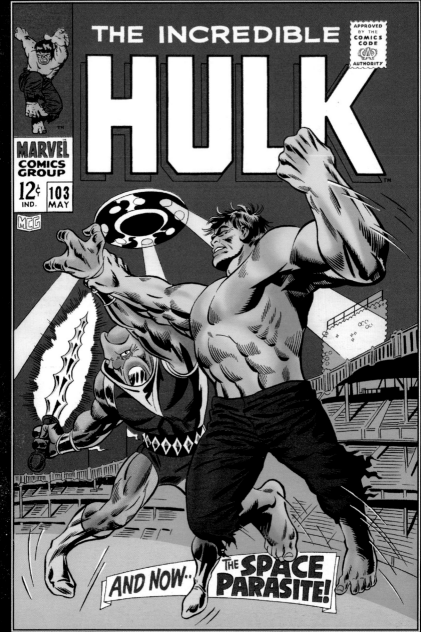

NOW HULK CAN SEE FOR *BLOCKS*... I'LL SEE THE ARMY BEFORE IT CAN SEE *ME!*

PUNY WEAKLINGS! BRING YOUR STRONGEST... YOUR BEST *SOLDIERS*... AND HULK WILL BEAT THEM *ALL!*

BUT, AT THAT EXACT INSTANT...

NOTHING CAN STOP... *=AAARRRHHH!=*

NOT... *NOW!* MUSTN'T CHANGE ...TOO WEAK... *BRUCE BANNER!*

HOWEVER, NOT EVEN THE FIERCE DETERMINATION OF THE *HULK* CAN PREVENT THE MOST AMAZING TRANSFORMATION SINCE *DOC JEKYLL* FROM OCCURRING...

NOOOOOOO!

IT'S... *TOO LATE!* I'M BECOMING...

BRUCE BANNER AGAIN.!

WHA...? I'M ON A NARROW LEDGE... HUNDREDS OF FEET ABOVE THE *GROUND!*

BUT HOW DID I *GET* HERE... AND WHY...?

I... MUST HAVE BEEN THE *HULK*... AND *LEAPED* HERE!

AND THAT MEANS PEOPLE MUST HAVE *SEEN* ME! THE *ARMY* WILL BE *HUNTING* ME!

I HAVE TO *GET AWAY*...

FIND A PLACE TO *HIDE*... TO *THINK!*

MUST *HURRY*, THOUGH! IF I'M SPOTTED, THEY MAY SHOOT ME ON *SIGHT!*

3.

BUT, WHILE THE SEEMINGLY ENDLESS GAME OF HIDE AND SEEK BEGINS ONCE MORE, LET'S TURN OUR ATTENTION TO A MIDTOWN *TELEVISION STUDIO* -- WHERE A POPULAR *TALK SHOW* IS NOW IN PROGRESS...

AND SO, ON BEHALF OF OUR SPONSOR, I'D NOW LIKE TO INTRODUCE OUR DISTINGUISHED *GUESTS* FOR TONIGHT...

GENERAL *THUNDERBOLT ROSS*, WHO IS IN CHARGE OF THE AIR FORCE'S CAMPAIGN TO *DESTROY* THE HULK... HIS SPECIAL AIDE, *MAJOR GLENN TALBOT*...

...AND THE YOUNG MAN WHO PROBABLY KNOWS MORE ABOUT THE GREEN-SKINNED NEMESIS THAN ANY-ONE ALIVE... *MR. RICK JONES!*

NEEDLESS TO SAY, OUR TOPIC FOR TONIGHT IS... *THE HULK!* SO, GENTLE-MEN, IF WE MAY... LET'S GET RIGHT DOWN TO THE *NITTY GRITTY,* AS THEY SAY!

TELL US, GENERAL ROSS... ISN'T IT TRUE THAT YOUR BATTLE WITH THE HULK HAS BEEN A TOTAL *FAILURE* TO THIS POINT?

NOW JUST A *SECOND,* KLYNE! PERHAPS YOU'RE JUST IGNORANT OF THE *FACTS!*

LIKE THE PUBLIC AS A WHOLE, YOU PROBABLY AREN'T AWARE OF THAT BEAST'S *STRENGTH!*

I'D SAY THAT'S PUTTING IT A LITTLE *STRONGLY,* MR. KLYNE! WE'VE ACTUALLY *SUCCEEDED* IN A NUMBER OF...

OH, COME NOW, GENERAL! DON'T TRY TO *CON* THE PUBLIC!

I HAVE SOME *FILM CLIPS* I'D LIKE TO SHOW WITH YOUR PERMISSION, THAT MAY OPEN YOUR *EYES* AS TO JUST WHY THE HULK IS STILL AT LARGE!

IN THIS SCENE, TAKEN ONLY A FEW *WEEKS* AGO -- THE HULK DESTROYS A FIFTY-STORY *BUILDING* WITH A SINGLE BLOW!

WE CAN *SEE* THAT, MAJOR -- BUT WE ALREADY *KNEW* HE WASN'T A 98-POUND *WEAKLING!*

I'M NOT *FINISHED* YET! HERE YOU SEE HIM GETTING THE BEST OF THE *THING!*

IF *THAT* DOESN'T PROVE HE'S NO ORDINARY MENACE...

WE *REALIZE* HE'S NOT ORDINARY, MAJOR -- BUT SURELY YOU DON'T CONSIDER THIS PROOF THAT HE'S *UNSTOPABLE?*

4

BUT, WHILE THE *TRIAL BY TUBE* CONTINUES...

I'VE MADE IT TO THE BASEMENT WITHOUT BEING *SEEN*...BUT I CAN'T *STAY* HERE INDEFINITELY!

I HAVE TO THINK OF SOMEWHERE TO *GO!*

UH OH! VOICES IN THE NEXT ROOM!

HAVE TO BE MORE *CAREFUL!* I ALMOST WALKED RIGHT *IN* ON THEM!

THEN, SECONDS LATER, THE DISTRAUGHT SCIENTIST FINDS MOMENTARY RESPITE IN A DESERTED *LOCKER ROOM*...

IF I GIVE MYSELF *UP*--I'LL PROBABLY BE LOCKED AWAY FOR *LIFE!*

YET, IF I *DON'T*, I'M CERTAIN TO BECOME THE *HULK* AGAIN...

...AND GOD ONLY *KNOWS* WHAT OR WHO I MIGHT *HARM!*

HOWEVER, THOUGH HE CANNOT KNOW IT, THINGS ARE DESTINED TO GET A LOT *WORSE* FOR THE TORTURED FUGITIVE...

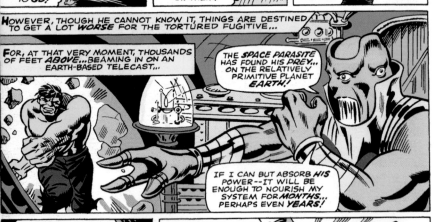

FOR, AT THAT VERY MOMENT, THOUSANDS OF FEET *ABOVE*...BEAMING IN ON AN EARTH-BASED TELECAST...

THE *SPACE PARASITE* HAS FOUND HIS PREY...ON THE RELATIVELY PRIMITIVE PLANET *EARTH!*

IF I CAN BUT ABSORB *HIS* POWER--IT WILL BE ENOUGH TO NOURISH MY SYSTEM FOR *MONTHS*... PERHAPS EVEN *YEARS!*

MY COURSE IS NOW SET FOR THE CITY EARTHLINGS CALL *NEW YORK!* THERE I WILL FIGHT MY GREATEST *BATTLE*...

...AND THERE I WILL WIN MY SWEETEST *VICTORY*...OVER THE GREEN-HUED GARGOYLE KNOWN ONLY AS... *THE HULK!*

FOR I WAS CREATED TO *DESTROY!* ONLY THROUGH THE DESTRUCTION OF *OTHERS* MAY I EXIST!

WHEN AN OPPONENT FALLS, HIS STRENGTH FLOWS INTO *ME*... AND BECOMES MY OWN *LIFE-BLOOD!*

SO IT HAS ALWAYS BEEN ...AND SO IT SHALL ALWAYS BE FOR... *THE SPACE PARASITE!*

5

AND, AS THE STRANGE SPACE-CRAFT HURTLES TOWARD **EARTH**...

I HAVE NO **RIGHT** TO INVOLVE HIM! I'VE CAUSED HIM TOO MUCH GRIEF **ALREADY**...

...BUT THERE'S NO ONE ELSE I CAN **TURN** TO!

IF I CAN JUST FIND **RICK JONES'** ADDRESS!

HOWEVER, SECONDS **LATER**...

HEY...**YOU!** WHAT'RE YOU DOIN' HERE AT THIS TIME'A NIGHT?

HOLD IT! COME BACK HERE!

GOT THE ADDRESS ...BUT HAVE TO LOSE THAT **GUARD!**

THANK HEAVENS THERE'S A **SUBWAY ENTRANCE** RIGHT OUTSIDE--

I DON'T HAVE A **TOKEN**...HOPE THE CHANGE CLERK DOESN'T...

59TH S

NOT AN EXIT

NOT AN EXIT

YOU... WAIT!

BUT, LUCK IS **WITH** THE NOW EXHAUSTED BRUCE BANNER--AND A TRAIN PULLS INTO THE STATION BEFORE THE TRANSIT POLICE CAN BE SUMMONED! THEN...

THAT WAS...**CLOSE!** WHAT **IRONY** IT WOULD HAVE BEEN...

...TO HAVE **ESCAPED** CAPTURE ALL THESE MONTHS--AND THEN GET CAUGHT BECAUSE I DON'T HAVE **TWENTY CENTS!**

MEANWHILE, THOUGH, A FAR MORE DEADLY MENACE THAN THE **LAW** IS DRAWING EVER **NEARER**...

THERE! I AM NOW WITHIN **TELEPORTATION DISTANCE** OF EARTH! I MUST STOP MY CRAFT--AND HOME IN ON MY **QUARRY!**

BUT...WHAT IS **THIS?** MY FINDER IS **BLANK!** THERE IS NO SIGN OF THE HULK!

AND THE SCANNER IS CONSTRUCTED TO FIND ANY OBJECT IT IS **TUNED** TO! THE ONLY WAY IT WILL NOT REGISTER...

...IS IF THE CHOSEN OBJECT DOES NOT **EXIST!**

WAIT! WHAT ARE THESE **MEN** I NOW SEE?

SUPPOSING YOU TELL US HOW **YOU** FEEL ABOUT THE HULK, MR. JONES?

DO YOU STILL CONTEND HE IS **NOT** A MENACE?

WELL, SIR... I...

5

[45]

BUT, FOR NOW, KEEP SCRIBBLING ON YOUR *SCORE CARDS*, 'CAUSE IT'S SCENE-SWITCHING TIME AGAIN...

DON'T GIVE ME THE *THIRD DEGREE*, WOMAN! I'M RICK JONES' UNCLE-- AND I WANT THE KEY TO HIS *APARTMENT!*

VERY WELL, YOUNG MAN --BUT IF YOU'RE *LYING*, YOU'LL GET *CAUGHT!* CRIME DOESN'T *PAY*, YOU KNOW!

THEN, MOMENTS LATER...

PERHAPS IT'S BETTER THAT RICK ISN'T *HOME!* NOW I'LL HAVE TIME TO...*WHAT'S THIS?*

A TV PROGRAM... WITH THE JACK KLYNE SHOW CIRCLED...AND IT SAYS RICK'S A *GUEST*...TO TALK ABOUT THE *HULK!*

IT'S ON RIGHT *NOW*--SO I MIGHT AS WELL HAVE A *LOOK!* IT'LL DO ME GOOD TO HEAR SOMEBODY SAY SOMETHING *KIND* ABOUT...

I NOW REALIZE THAT THERE'S NO *HOPE* FOR THE HULK! WHEN HE *TURNED* ON ME...

...I WAS FINALLY CONVINCED THAT HE'S A *MENACE*... AND THAT HE MUST BE *DESTROYED!*

FOR LONG, OMINOUSLY SILENT MINUTES, THE ANGUISHED SCIENTIST SITS STUNNED, UNBELIEVING-- AND MORE *ALONE* THAN ANY MAN HAS EVER BEEN!

UNTIL, FINALLY...

I--I CAN'T *STAY* HERE! RICK WOULD TURN ME *IN* IF HE FOUND ME!

I JUST HEARD THE WORDS FROM HIS OWN *LIPS!* I MUST *LEAVE*... BEFORE HE ARRIVES!

BUT... WHERE WILL I...

HOLD IT, BRUCE! DON'T MAKE ME *SHOOT* YOU!

RICK...YOU... YOU'RE HOLDING A *GUN* ON ME!

I HEARD WHAT YOU SAID ON *TELEVISION* --AND I UNDERSTAND HOW YOU *FEEL!*

BUT YOU SURELY WOULDN'T PULL THAT *TRIGGER*-- NOT ON THE MAN WHO ONCE SAVED YOUR *LIFE!*

7

YOU...YOU'RE DEAD *WRONG*, BRUCE! I HAVE NO *CHOICE!*

AS LONG AS THERE'S ANY CHANCE OF YOU TURNING INTO THE *HULK* AGAIN...

...YOU'RE A DEADLY *MENACE!*

"EVEN NOW, THE ENTIRE CITY IS *LOOKING* FOR YOU...*HUNTING* YOU...HOPING TO *DESTROY* YOU! AND, FOR THE SAKE OF ALL MANKIND--THAT'S WHAT THEY *MUST DO!*"

"THEY CAN'T AFFORD TO RISK LETTING YOU BECOME THE HULK AGAIN...*EVER!*"

AND, AT THAT SAME MOMENT, HIGH ABOVE THE BRIGHTLY-LIT *CITY*...

SO *THAT* IS THE ANSWER...BRUCE BANNER AND THE HULK ARE ONE AND THE *SAME!*

WHICH MEANS I MUST *FACE* BANNER--AND SOMEHOW TURN HIM BACK INTO... *THE HULK!*

WHILE...

JUST *STAY BACK*...PLEASE DON'T COME ANY *CLOSER!*

DON'T MAKE ME SHOOT! LET ME CALL THE *POLICE*... *PLEASE!*

YOU DON'T KNOW WHAT YOU'RE *SAYING!* YOU COULDN'T CONDEMN ME TO *DEATH*...

...ANY MORE THAN YOU COULD SHOOT ME DOWN IN *COLD BLOOD!* NOW HAND ME THE *GUN!*

BUT, AS BRUCE BANNER INCHES EVER CLOSER TO HIS TORMENTED YOUNG *CAPTOR*...

I JUST CAN'T *BELIEVE* RICK HAS TURNED AGAINST BRUCE!

SOMEONE MUST HAVE *FORCED* HIM TO SAY THOSE TERRIBLE THINGS, ON TV!

IF HE *DOES* MEAN IT, THOUGH...I MUST HEAR IT FROM HIM IN *PERSON!*

RICK, I'M SORRY TO *BARGE* IN LIKE...

RICK! NOOOOO!

KRAK

BRUCE...DARLING! ARE YOU...

I COULDN'T...*DO* IT! I JUST COULDN'T MAKE MYSELF *HARM* HIM!

I FIRED INTO THE *FLOOR*...AT THE LAST SECOND!

I'M *ALL RIGHT*, BETTY --BUT YOU SHOULDN'T HAVE *COME* HERE!

THE ENTIRE POLICE FORCE IS *SEARCHING* FOR ME--AND YOUR FATHER PROBABLY HAS THE *AIR FORCE* AFTER ME, TOO!

IF THEY SHOULD LEARN I'M *HERE*...

I'VE FAILED MY *COUNTRY* ...AND MYSELF!

THAT DOESN'T *MATTER*, DARLING! I'M NOT *AFRAID*...

I *COULDN'T* BE, AS LONG AS I'M WITH THE MAN I...

THEN, *SUDDENLY*...

BETTY... WHAT IS IT?

YOU...YOU'RE A *KILLER*! YOU SHOULD BE...YOU MUST BE... *DESTROYED*!

HELLLPP!!

PERFECT! EXCELLENT! I'VE SUCCEEDED IN PROJECTING A HYPNOTIC SUGGESTION INTO THE GIRL'S BRAIN--VIA *LASER BEAM*!

NOW, IF ONLY THE SHOCK OF HER CHANGE WILL CAUSE BANNER TO BECOME *THE HULK*!

THE BATTLE CAN AT LAST BEGIN!

I MUST RUSH TO THE *TELEPORTATION CHAMBER*...SO THAT I WILL BE *PRESENT* WHEN THE HULK WALKS THE EARTH ONCE MORE!

THEN, WITHIN THE MEREST *MICROSECOND*, THE ALIEN BEING IS HURLED THROUGH SPACE AT A SPEED FASTER THAN *LIGHT*...

...HURTLING TOWARD A DEADLY CLASH WHICH MAY WELL CHANGE THE DESTINY OF ALL *MANKIND*!

9

UNTIL... *BEGONE*, PUNY EARTHLING...AND SUMMON FORTH THE GREEN-SKINNED GARGOYLE I COME TO *CONQUER!*

SUCH IS THE AWESOME CHALLENGE OF...*THE SPACE PARASITE!*

I DON'T KNOW *WHO* YOU ARE...OR WHAT YOU *WANT*...

BUT I CAN'T BECOME THE HULK *AT WILL!*

MY PULSE... SUDDENLY *POUNDING!* HEAD... STARTING TO *SPIN!*

I MUSTN'T BECOME THE HULK *NOW,* THOUGH...NOT WITH *BETTY* HERE!

NO *USE...* CAN'T *HELP* MYSELF!

NO WAY TO *STOP* IT!

ONCE AGAIN I'VE BECOME...

THE HULK!

AT LAST! I AM FACE TO FACE WITH THE ONE FOE WHO CAN ASSURE MY EXISTENCE FOR *COUNTLESS YEARS!*

FOLLOW ME, YOU AWESOME ABOMINATION-- THAT WE MAY MEET ON A FITTING *BATTLEGROUND!*

HULK WILL *FOLLOW!* AND HULK WILL *CRUSH* YOU!

10

YOU CAN'T RUN AWAY FROM *HULK!*

EVEN IN THE *AIR*-- THERE'S NO WAY YOU CAN *ESCAPE* ME!

THWAKOW!

YOUR BRAVERY IN ACCEPTING MY CHALLENGE IS *ADMIRABLE...*

...BUT IT WILL BRING ABOUT YOUR INEVITABLE *DOOM!*

EVEN *NOW* THE RAYS OF MY *SOLAR SCEPTER* BEGIN TO SAP THE STRENGTH FROM YOUR BODY!

BUT...WHAT IS *THIS?* THE SOLAR BLASTS ONLY *STUNNED* YOU!

ARRRGGGHHHH!

IN THE PAST, RAYS OF SUCH INTENSITY WOULD TOTALLY DRAIN THE POWER OF A *HUNDRED MEN!*

HULK IS STRONGER THAN A *THOUSAND MEN!* NO PUNY WEAPON CAN STOP ME!

THEN LET OUR BATTLE BE ONE OF SHEER, BRUTE *FORCE...*

...FOR BY MERELY *TOUCHING* YOU, I CAN TRANSFER THE POWER WHICH COURSES THROUGH YOUR BODY...

...INTO *MINE!*

HOWEVER, AS THE TWO MIGHTY TITANS CLASH OVER THE ROOFTOPS OF *NEW YORK...*

...THEY ARE WATCHED WITH INTENSE CONCERN FROM MILLIONS OF MILES AWAY ON THE *PLANET XERON...*

WE HAVE FOUND HIM...AT LAST! EVEN TO THIS DAY... *RANDAU LIVES!*

YES...JUST AS WE HAVE *FEARED* FOR THESE MANY YEARS!

BUT, NOW THAT WE *HAVE* LOCATED HIM... WHAT CAN WE *DO* ABOUT IT?

11

THAT SHOULD BE *OBVIOUS*, EXCELLENCY!

RANDAU MUST BE... *DESTROYED!*

CAN YOU SPEAK SO *CASUALLY* ABOUT KILLING HIM WE ONCE CALLED *KING?*

I *CAN-- NOT!*

"TOO WELL DO I REMEMBER THE DAY WHEN RANDAU *RULED* OVER THE PERFECT XERONIAN SOCIETY..."

"PERFECT, THAT IS, UNTIL THAT FATEFUL DAY WHEN..."

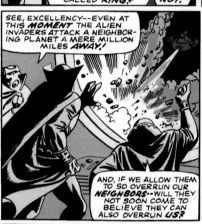

SEE, EXCELLENCY--EVEN AT THIS *MOMENT* THE ALIEN INVADERS ATTACK A NEIGHBORING PLANET A MERE MILLION MILES *AWAY!*

AND, IF WE ALLOW THEM TO SO OVERRUN OUR *NEIGHBORS*--WILL THEY NOT SOON COME TO BELIEVE THEY CAN ALSO OVERRUN *US?*

ENOUGH, MY ADVISORS! THOUGH I BE A MAN OF *PEACE*...I CAN-NOT STAND IDLY BY AND SEE THE SECURITY OF MY PEOPLE *THREATENED!*

PREPARE THE *SOLAR CHAMBER!*

BUT, EXCELLENCY--IT IS AS YET *UNTESTED!* WE DO NOT KNOW WHAT *EFFECTS* IT MAY HAVE UPON A LIVING BODY!

"HOWEVER, FULLY AWARE OF THE *GRAVE RISK* INVOLVED RANDAU ENTERED THE SOLAR CHAMBER.."

"AND ALLOWED HIS BODY TO BE BATHED IN THE MYSTERIOUS RAYS OF RANDAU'S *THIRD SUN!*"

"THEN, WHEN HE *EMERGED* FROM THE CHAMBER..."

WE HAVE *SUCCEEDED!* I CAN FEEL THE TOTAL ENERGY OF THE *UNI-VERSE* COURSING THROUGH MY *BODY!*

TAKE ME TO THE *ENEMIES* OF XERON--AND I SHALL *CRUSH* THEM!

IT--IT *WORKED!* RANDAU APPEARS TO HAVE BECOME A--A *LIVING WEAPON!*

YES, YOU FOOLS--AND HE HAS LIKEWISE BEEN CONVERTED FROM A JUST MONARCH OF *PEACE*--TO A HATE-FILLED *CONQUEROR!*

"BUT, OF COURSE, NO ONE WOULD LISTEN TO THE WORDS OF A DOVE-LIKE *OLD MAN*..."

"INSTEAD, THEY ALLOWED THEMSELVES TO BE FILLED WITH THE ALL-CONSUMING LUST FOR *WAR* AND *DEATH*--

HAVE NO FEAR, MY PEOPLE! ON THIS DAY, RANDAU STRIKES FOR *XERON*... THAT IT MAY NEVER KNOW THE FEAR OF INVASION *AGAIN!*

"AND, INDEED, RANDAU MADE GOOD HIS PROMISE! THE ENEMY WHICH ATTACKED XERON'S NEIGHBOR WAS MET AND *DESTROYED* BY HIM..."

"HOWEVER, WITH EVERY VICTORY, THE *STRENGTH* OF RANDAU SEEMED TO INCREASE A THOUSANDFOLD..."

"THEN, WHEN THE FINAL BATTLE WAS ENDED, RANDAU FOUND HE COULD NOT *STOP!* THOUGH HIS PEOPLE HAD BEEN SAVED--HIS THIRST FOR BATTLE LINGERED ON..."

"AND, INSTEAD OF *RETURNING*, HE CONTINUED ON AN ENDLESS QUEST FOR YET ANOTHER LIFE-GIVING SIP FROM THE VAT OF *BATTLE!*"

"...LEAVING BEHIND ONLY A *MESSAGE* WHICH PROVED UNACCEPTABLE TO MOST XERONIANS!"

HEAR THIS, MY PEOPLE! RANDAU CONTINUES ON INTO THE UNKNOWN --FAR *BEYOND* THIS UNIVERSE OF OURS...

FOR SPACE IS *FILLED* WITH MENACES TO OUR PLANET-- AND RANDAU WILL NOT REST UNTIL THEY ALL HAVE BEEN *STAMPED OUT!*

"SO, FOR COUNTLESS YEARS SINCE, HE HAS ROAMED THE *HEAVENS* THEM-SELVES--CONQUERING NEW *FOES* AT EACH STOP ALONG THE WAY..."

"UNTIL, TODAY, WE HAVE FINALLY COME TO REALIZE THAT HE FIGHTS *NOT* FOR XERON-- BUT TO FULFILL HIS *OWN* BODILY NEEDS..."

"...A NEED WHICH COMMANDS THE FRESH STRENGTH OF A FOE BE ABSORBED INTO HIS BODY AT FREQUENT INTERVALS..."

"...FOR THERE IS NO OTHER WAY HE CAN *SURVIVE!*"

AH...THROUGH MY OWN *REMEMBRANCES* I HAVE FOUND THE ANSWER WE SEEK!

EVEN THOUGH ONCE RANDAU MAY HAVE *SAVED* US--HE NOW IS THE PERSONIFICATION OF ALL THAT OUR PEOPLE *DESPISE... HATE, WAR, AND DEATH!*

OUR COURSE OF ACTION IS *CLEAR...*

...*RANDAU MUST DIE!*

13

BUT, WHILE THE XERONIANS PREPARE TO MAKE A FATEFUL *MOVE*, LET'S SEE WHAT'S HAPPENING BACK ON THE *NEW YORK SCENE...*

HULK... LOSING GRIP!

GOING TO FALL... BACK TO EARTH!

AND FALL THE JOLLY GREEN GOLIATH *DOES--*AND HE LANDS, WOULD'JA BELIEVE RIGHT IN THE GOVERNOR'S BOX AT *YANKEE STADIUM!**

THWUMP!

*BREATHE EASY, YANK FANS! MICKEY MANTLE AND COMPANY ARE BUSILY ENGAGED AT *SHEA STADIUM* IN THE MAYOR'S-TROPHY GAME WITH THE METS.--SUPER-FAN STAN.

IT IS UNBELIEVABLE! YOU ARE NOT FAZED BY A FALL OF SEVERAL HUNDRED *FEET!*

BUT, EVEN STRENGTH AS REMARKABLE AS *YOURS* SHALL AVAIL YOU *NAUGHT!*

CRACK!

FOR NOW I SHALL SUMMON ALL MY *MIGHT* TO STRIKE A BLOW WHICH IS CERTAIN TO *STUN* YOU!

¡UUNNNHHHH!

THAT WAS NO MORE THAN A HARMLESS *BEE STING* TO HULK!

BUT NOW HULK IS TIRED OF PLAYING *GAMES!* NOW THE HULK WILL *ATTACK!*

THEN, AS THE STUNNED XERONIAN TUMBLES BACKWARD...

HAH! ONE LITTLE *BLOW* IS ENOUGH TO DEFEAT YOU!

RAAAKK!

BUT HULK WON'T TAKE ANY *CHANCES!*

HULK WILL MAKE *SURE* YOU DON'T BOTHER HIM AGAIN!

THOOM!

14

HULK WILL *BURY* YOU UNDER A MOUNTAIN OF *DEBRIS...*

...BEFORE YOU CAN RISE TO *ATTACK* HIM AGAIN!

THERE! NOTHING COULD SURVIVE THAT...EXCEPT THE *HULK!*

BLASH!

BUT, LIKE THE MAN SAID, "HOW WRONG CAN A HULK *BE?*"

LIKE ALL MY *PAST FOES,* YOU HAVE MADE THE GRAVE MISTAKE OF AROUSING MY *WRATH!*

THE GAME IS *ENDED!* NOW I WILL *ANNIHILATE* YOU!

EVERY TIME YOU *STRIKE* ME MORE OF YOUR STRENGTH BECOMES MY *OWN...*

...AND SO SHALL IT *CONTINUE*--UNTIL YOU ARE REDUCED TO *HELPLESSNESS!*

WHAAM!

AND NOW, WITH THIS REMAINING TIP OF MY *SCEPTER,* I SHALL DRAIN YOUR VERY *LIFEBLOOD!*

YOU WERE A VALOROUS *FOE*--BUT NO MATCH FOR... *THE SPACE PARASITE!*

HOWEVER, AT THAT SAME MOMENT, BACK ON THE PLANET *XERON...*

OBSERVE, EXCELLENCY! RANDAU IS ABOUT TO SLAY YET *ANOTHER* FOE!

THE SELF-DESTRUCT MECHANISM ON HIS SHIP CAN NOW BE DETONATED BY *US!*

AS SOON AS HE *RETURNS* TO IT-- EXCELLENCY, DO YOU NOT *HEAR* ME?

15

BUT, WE AREN'T DESTINED TO KNOW THE TROUBLED XERONIAN MONARCH'S ANSWER... *YET!*

BECAUSE, FOR NOW, THE *"HOUSE THAT RUTH BUILT"* IS *WHERE THE ACTION IS...*

YOU STILL THINK MERE *GADGETS* CAN DEFEAT HULK?

NO... IT ISN'T *POSSIBLE!* I'M CONCENTRATING THE SCEPTOR'S ENTIRE *ENERGY SOURCE* ON HIM...

...AND HE'S STILL COMING *AT* ME!

HOWEVER, IN THE COURSE OF THE BATTLE, THE POWER LINES WHICH SUPPLY ELECTRICITY TO THE NEARBY TRACKS OF THE ELEVATED *IRT SUBWAY LINE* HAVE BEEN SEVERED, AND...

EVACUATE THE TRAIN!

DON'T *PUSH,* LADY! *EVERYBODY* WANTS TO GET AWAY FROM THE HULK!

MY... STRENGTH IS... *FADING!*

IT'S BEEN TOO LONG,... SINCE I DRAINED A VICTIM OF HIS... *ENERGY!*

NOW HULK WILL SHOW YOU THE TRUE *MEANING* OF...

DEFEAT!

BRASH!

I CANNOT HOLD OUT MUCH *LONGER!* GETTING... WEAKER EVERY *SECOND!*

MUST CONCENTRATE EVERYTHING ON ONE, FINAL... *ATTACK!*

SURELY, IF I DROP THIS MASSIVE PIECE OF CRUDE *MACHINERY* ON HIM...

YOU *STILL* LIVE? YOU DARE TO KEEP *FIGHTING* HULK?

16

LOOK! UP THERE ON THE ELEVATED!

IT'S THE HULK!! ...FIGHTING WITH SOME HUGE, ONE-EYED MONSTER!

MOVE THOSE TANKS IN... ON THE DOUBLE!

I...WASN'T FAST ENOUGH! HE SEES ME...

...AND HE'S MOVING TO MEET MY ATTACK!

I'M TOO WEAK... TO HURL THE MACHINERY!

BRAK!!

NO ONE RISES AFTER HULK HAS DOWNED HIM... AND LIVES!

GET UP! WHY DON'T YOU ATTACK ME AGAIN? HAS HULK FINALLY GOT THE BEST OF YOU?

TOO WEAK...TO STAND! AND HE'S...COMING STRAIGHT FOR ME!

CAN THIS BE...THE BITTER TASTE OF... DEFEAT?

YOU DON'T WANT TO FIGHT ANY MORE? THAT'S FINE WITH HULK!

NOW HULK MAKE SURE YOU NEVER BOTHER HIM AGAIN!

KE-RUNCH!

I'LL WRAP YOU IN THIS TRAIN CAR...

EXPRESS

...LEAP HIGH INTO THE AIR...

...AS ONLY THE HULK CAN DO!

THEN DUMP THE REMAINS INTO THE RIVER!

NOW HULK HAS SEEN THE LAST OF YOU!

GZWOING!

17

BUT, AS THE MANGLED MASS OF STEEL SINKS SLOWLY TOWARD THE RIVER'S *BOTTOM*...

BEING ENGULFED BY *WATER*...HAVE TO BREAK *FREE!*

MUSTN'T DIE *THIS* WAY!

THEN, SUMMONING EVERY BIT OF STRENGTH THAT REMAINS WITHIN HIS FATIGUED BEING, THE SPACE PARASITE STRAINS AGAINST THE METAL *PRISON*...

I AM *KING*...CANNOT DIE...EXCEPT IN...*BATTLE!*

STRENGTH...NEARLY GONE --BUT, THE METAL IS...*GIVING!*

I HAVE *DONE* IT! I AM *FREE*...

...FREE TO DIE...LIKE A WARRIOR *BORN!*

HOWEVER, AS THE CREATURE FROM THE FARTHEST REACHES OF OUTER SPACE *SURFACES*...

CAN'T MOVE...ANOTHER *INCH!* DEATH...VERY NEAR!

MUST FALL...BY THE HAND OF THE ONE WHO *CONQUERED* ME--!

WHAT? HOW DID YOU *ESCAPE?* HOW COULD...

HEAR ME...*EARTHLING!* YOU HAVE...*VANQUISHED* ME! NOW ACCORD ME THE HONOR TO...DIE IN...*COMBAT!*

WHAT? STRIKE ONE WHO'S WEAK...CAN'T FIGHT *BACK?*

NO! HULK ONLY FIGHTS THOSE THAT *THREATEN* HIM!

THEN,...I MUST RETURN...TO MY *SHIP!* AT LEAST...I CAN DIE...ON *HOME SOIL!*

AND, WITH BUT A TOUCH OF HIS TELEPORTATION UNIT, THE BODY OF THE SPACE PARASITE FADES FROM *VIEW!*

AND, EVEN AS HIS FORMER KING HURTLES THROUGH SPACE TOWARD HIS ORBITING CRAFT--THE RULER OF **XERON** PREPARES TO ACT...

THE MOMENT IS AT **HAND!** I NOW PRESS THE DETONATOR WHICH WILL DESTROY THE SHIP...AND **RANDAU!**

MAY THE GODS **FORGIVE** ME!

YOU CAN BE SURE THAT THEY **WILL**, EXCELLENCY! YOU DO WHAT HAS TO BE **DONE!**

THEN, WITHIN A MICROSECOND, HIGH ABOVE THE **EARTH**...

BARROOOM!

HOWEVER, UNKNOWN TO THE XERONIANS, THE OBJECT OF THE ACTION WAS IN TELEPORTATIONAL TRAVEL AT THE MOMENT OF THE **EXPLOSION**--

SHIP... EXPLODED!

MY PEOPLE...MUST HAVE...**LOCATED** ME...AND ATTEMPTED TO...**DESTROY** ME!

NOWHERE TO **GO**...NOW! NO **HOME** TO... RETURN TO!

NOTHING LEFT... BUT...

SO...**TIRED** ...WEAK!

DEATH... SO **NEAR!**

THOUGH I AM TOTALLY... **ALONE**...

AT LEAST SOON...I SHALL ONCE AGAIN KNOW...THE MEANING OF...

...**PEACE!**

19

AND, AT THAT VERY MOMENT, THERE IS AT LEAST *ONE* WHO WOULD LIKEWISE WISH TO KNOW PEACE...

HOLD IT RIGHT THERE, HULK! WE HAVE YOU SURROUNDED! DON'T TRY TO ESCAPE!

THE POLICE...AFTER ME *AGAIN!* WHY CAN'T THEY *LEARN*...

THE HULK CAN NEVER BE CAPTURED!

LOOK OUT! HE LOOKS LIKE HE'S GONNA JUMP!

HURL THOSE TEAR GAS GRENADES!

OOOF!

WISSH!

THIS OUGHTTA HOLD 'IM TILL THE ARMY GETS HERE!

KEEP MOVIN' *IN* ON 'IM, JOE! WE GOTTA MAKE SURE HE'S *HELPLESS!*

IF HE *ISN'T*, I'VE GOT ENOUGH GAS IN THIS TANK TO STOP AN *ELEPHANT!*

YEAH...BUT IS IT ENOUGH TO STOP THE *HULK?*

20

BUT, AS THE MASKED POLICEMEN REACH THE SPOT WHERE THE HULK WAS LAST SEEN *STANDING*...

HE'S CHANGED BACK TO BANNER!

PUT 'EM UP HIGH, BUDDY.

DON'T LOOK NOW, BUT IT'S...

TO BE HULKWUED

TIME AGAIN!!!

[59]

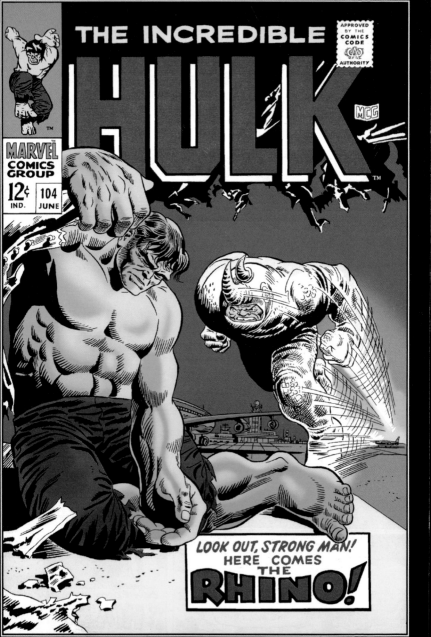

AND, WHILE THE WORLD READS THE STARTLING NEWS OF THE HULK'S CAPTURE OVER COFFEE AND TOASTED ENGLISH MUFFINS, LET US TURN OUR ATTENTION TO *SING-SING PRISON...*

IS THIS HOW IT WILL *END*? WILL I NEVER AGAIN KNOW THE SWEET SMELL OF CLEAN, FRESH *AIR*?

AM I DOOMED TO SPEND THE REST OF MY LIFE LIKE A *CAGED ANIMAL*?

WHILE, JUST OUTSIDE THE *CELL DOOR...*

NO, I DON'T HAVE ANY ANSWERS AS TO WHAT WE'LL *DO* WITH HIM, *TALBOT!*

LET'S GO *TALK* TO HIM!

THEN, AS *GENERAL THUNDER-BOLT ROSS* AND *MAJOR GLENN TALBOT* ENTER BRUCE BANNER'S CELL...

GENERAL... YOU MUST *LISTEN* TO ME!

YOU CAN'T *KEEP* ME HERE...

...UNDER THE INFLUENCE OF *SEDATIVES!*

I THINK I KNOW A WAY TO *SAVE* MYSELF!

YOU HAVE TO TAKE ME TO MY *LAB...* YOU *MUST!*

HOLD IT, BANNER! CALM DOWN! THERE'S NO WAY YOU CAN *ESCAPE!*

YOU *FOOLS!* I DON'T WANT TO ESCAPE! I'M *TIRED* OF RUNNING!

GIVE HIM ANOTHER *SHOT* ...*QUICKLY!* HE'S TOO UPSET..MIGHT CHANGE TO THE *HULK!*

THIS SHOULD CALM HIM DOWN, MAJOR!

HOWEVER, EVEN AS THE FLUID REACHES THE TORMENTED *BRAIN* OF THE BRILLIANT SCIENTIST, CAUSING HIM TO CRUMPLE TO THE *FLOOR...*

YOU MUST...*LISTEN* TO ME.! I THINK... I KNOW A WAY TO...PREVENT ME FROM...EVER *BECOMING...* THE HULK AGAIN!

SORRY, BANNER... BUT WE CAN'T TAKE THE RISK! AS LONG AS WE KEEP YOU UNDER SEDATION...WE *KNOW* YOU CAN'T CHANGE TO THAT GREEN-SKINNED MENACE!

BUT...IF ONLY ...YOU'D LET..ME... *TRY!* GETTING... SO...*SLEEPY!* I...

2.

BUT, AS THE POWERFUL DRUG OVERCOMES BANNER'S WILL TO REMAIN *CONSCIOUS* ...

...LET'S SEE WHAT WE CAN GET SHAKING *VILLAIN-WISE* ...

WHAT'RE YOU GUYS *WAITIN'* FOR? I COULD DIE OF *OLD AGE* BEFORE YOU GET FINISHED AT THE RATE YOU'RE *GOIN'!*

PATIENCE ...*PLEASE!* IT WILL ONLY BE A FEW MINUTES *MORE* ...

BEFORE *THE RHINO* SHALL AGAIN WALK THE *EARTH!*

PROMISES, PROMISES! *HURRY IT UP,* HUH?

"BUT IT SEEMS LIKE *TEN YEARS AGO* THAT I FIRST GOT OUTTA PRISON! *"

AHHH, I WAITED *THREE MONTHS!* I DON'T GUESS A COUPL'A MORE *MINUTES* IS GONNA KILL ME!

HOW CAN A GUY WHO USED TO BE *THE RHINO* GO TO BEIN' NOTHIN' BUT A CRUMMY *EX-CON?*

SO YER A *FREE MAN* AGAIN? SO *WHAT?* YOU AIN'T GOT NOTHIN' GOIN' FOR YA BUT YER *PRISON RECORD!*

*AND WE ALL KNOW WHAT FRIENDLY, NEIGHBORHOOD WEB-SPINNER *PUT* HIM THERE! RIGHT! RIGHT! ...*SURE-FIRE STAN.*

"BUT, A FEW MINUTES LATER, THERE WUZ A *KNOCK* AT MY DOOR, AND..."

YOU SEEM *SURPRISED!*

DIDN'T YOU *EXPECT* TO EVER AGAIN MEET THOSE WHO GAVE YOU YOUR *FORMER STRENGTH?*

AND WE'VE COME NOT FOR *REVENGE--* BUT TO OFFER YOU ...*THIS!*

YER TALKIN' MY *LANGUAGE!* C'MON IN... BUT DON'T TRY NUTHIN' JUST 'CAUSE I *DOUBLE-CROSSED* YOU BEFORE!

"THEN, THEY TOLD ME THERE WASN'T NO *HARD FEELIN'S...* AND THAT THEY WANTED TO MAKE ME *THE RHINO* AGAIN..."

LOOK! THIS FILM SHOULD REMIND YOU OF HOW *POWERFUL* YOU ONCE WERE!

AND YOU CAN BE THAT STRONG ONCE *MORE*...IF YOU'LL ACCEPT OUR *PROPOSAL!*

SINCE I WASN'T IN NO POSITION TO *REFUSE,* I WENT ALONG WITH THE CREEPS!

AND NOW, IN A FEW MORE SECONDS, I'M GONNA TAKE A *SECOND SHOT* AT BEIN THE *RHINO!*

THE PROCESS IS *FINISHED!* YOU MAY *COME DOWN* NOW!

YOU TALKED ME *INTO IT!*

3.

GOOD! THEN WATCH THESE FILMS... SHOWING *THE HULK* IN ACTION!

DO YOU FEEL YOU ARE STRONG ENOUGH TO DEFEAT EVEN *HIM*?

KEEP IN MIND THAT HE IS THE MOST POWERFUL BEING KNOWN TO *MAN*!

IF YOU *CAN* DEFEAT HIM... IT WOULD MEAN *THE RHINO* BECOMES THE STRONGEST BEING ALIVE!

BAH! I CAN CRUSH HIM AS EASY AS I CAN RIP THIS *SCREEN* TO SHREDS! MAYBE EVEN *EASIER*!

I WUZ *STUPID* WHEN I LET SPIDER-MAN BEAT ME... BUT THAT'LL NEVER HAPPEN AGAIN! JUST TELL ME WHERE TO *FIND* THE HULK... AND I'LL TEAR 'IM APART WITH MY BARE *HANDS*! HE'S AS GOOD AS DEAD RIGHT *NOW*!

RRIPP!

BUT, AT THAT SAME MOMENT, THE HULK IS VERY MUCH *ALIVE*... AT LEAST IN THE TORMENTED DREAMS OF *BRUCE BANNER*...

NO!

GO AWAY!

WHY MUST YOU *HAUNT* ME?

WHY CAN'T YOU LEAVE ME IN *PEACE*? WHY... WHY...

WHHHYYYY?

5.

HURRY UP...MOVE HIM OUT! WE CAN'T BE SLOWED UP BECAUSE HE'S HAVING *NIGHTMARES!*

GET HIM INTO THE AMBULANCE AS QUICKLY AS *POSSIBLE!* WE'RE DUE AT *JFK AIRPORT* IN TWO HOURS!

AND HE MAY WAKE UP AT ANY...

BRUCE...BRUCE *DARLING!* WHAT HAVE THEY *DONE* TO YOU? OH, *FATHER...* HOW *COULD* YOU?

I *LOVE* THIS MAN...AND YOU'RE TREATING HIM AS THOUGH HE WERE...A DANGEROUS WILD *BEAST!*

BETTY! WHAT ARE *YOU* DOING *HERE?* THERE'S NOTHING YOU CAN DO TO *HELP* HIM!

BUT... YOU KNOW HOW MUCH I *CARE* FOR HIM! AT LEAST LET ME RIDE TO THE *AIRPORT* WITH HIM!

SURELY YOU CAN LET ME SPEND A FEW LAST MINUTES WITH THE ONLY MAN I'LL EVER *LOVE!*

ALL RIGHT! BUT IT WON'T BE *PLEASANT!* HE'S TO BE CONFINED IN A HIGH-SECURITY *PRISON* FOR THE PRESENT--

...AND THERE'S NOTHING YOU CAN DO TO *CHANGE* THAT!

THEN, AS THE UNCONSCIOUS SCIENTIST IS TAKEN TO A WAITING *AMBULANCE,* AN ANXIETY-WRACKED *RICK JONES* WATCHES THE PROCEEDINGS FROM HIS *EAST VILLAGE APARTMENT...*

I KNOW THIS IS ALL FOR THE *BEST...* AND STILL IT TEARS ME *APART* TO SEE BRUCE HAULED AWAY LIKE A *MURDERER!*

I'M SURE THERE'S NOTHING I CAN *DO* AT THIS STAGE... BUT SOMETHING TELLS ME I JUST HAVE TO GO TO THE AIRPORT AND *SEE* HIM ONE LAST TIME!

MAYBE I CAN AT LEAST MAKE HIM *UNDERSTAND* WHY I TURNED AGAINST HIM... AND ASK HIM TO *FORGIVE* ME!

THEN, AT THAT SAME MOMENT, ONLY A FEW BLOCKS AWAY...

ACTUALLY, IT'S *BRUCE BANNER* THAT WE WANT! OUR ORGANIZATION COULD MAKE GREAT USE OF A MAN WITH HIS EXTENSIVE KNOWLEDGE OF *GAMMA RAYS!*

THEREFORE, YOUR REAL TASK IS TO CAPTURE BANNER... BUT YOU MUST BE PREPARED TO BATTLE *THE HULK*... IN CASE HE CHANGES BEFORE YOU CAN *BRING* HIM TO US!

BUT, DO NOT FORGET THAT YOUR COSTUME IS EQUIPPED WITH A *DESTRUCT DEVICE*... IN CASE YOU SHOULD DECIDE TO *TURN* ON US AGAIN!

CLICK

DON'T *SWEAT* IT, JACK! THIS TIME I *KNOW* I NEED YOUR BRAINS TO GO ALONG WITH MY *MUSCLE!*

AND NOW, ALL I CAN SAY IS-- GET A *WELCOMING PARTY* READY FOR BANNER...

'CAUSE I'LL BE *BACK* WITH HIM IN NO TIME FLAT!

AND, IN THE MEANTIME, A HEAVILY-ESCORTED AMBULANCE PULLS ONTO *LONG ISLAND EXPRESSWAY*, ONLY A FEW MILES FROM THE *JOHN F. KENNEDY INTERNATIONAL AIRPORT...*

MAN, I'LL SURE BE GLAD WHEN WE GET BANNER ON A *PLANE*... AND OUTTA OUR *HAIR!*

I DON'T MIND A LITTLE *HAZARDOUS DUTY*... BUT GUARDIN' THE *HULK* IS LIKE SITTIN' ON A KEG OF *NITRO!*

WHILE, *INSIDE* THE SPEEDING VEHICLE...

WHY MUST YOU SIT THERE WITH THAT *NEEDLE* AIMED AT HIM... AS THOUGH YOU WERE GUARDING A CRIMINAL WITH A *GUN?*

JUST DOING MY *JOB*, MAN! I DON'T MEAN ANY *OFFENSE!*

GOOD LORD-- WHAT A *NIGHTMARE!* IF ONLY CONGRESS WOULD GIVE US THE WORD TO *DESTROY* HIM... THEN ALL THIS COULD FINALLY *END!*

I FEEL THE SAME *WAY*... BUT IS THAT HOW I WANT TO *WIN* BETTY'S LOVE... THROUGH THE DEATH OF THE MAN SHE *REALLY* CARES FOR?

7.

AND, AS THE MOST *UNBELIEVABLE* HEIST SINCE THE *GREAT BOSTON MAIL ROBBERY* IS TAKING PLACE...

THIS IS A BULLETIN! THE AMBULANCE CARRYING BRUCE BANNER HAS BEEN ATTACKED AT JFK AIRPORT! STAY TUNED FOR FURTHER DEVELOPMENTS!

I SHOULD HAVE KNOWN SOMETHING WOULD HAPPEN! I WAS *DRIVEN* HERE BY SOME STRANGE *IMPULSE!*

LUCKILY, I'M ONLY A *COUPLE'A* MINUTES *AWAY!* MAYBE I CAN DO SOMETHING WHEN I *GET* THERE!

WHILE, AT THE *AIRPORT...*

OUR *BULLETS--* DON'T DO ANY *GOOD!*

THEY JUST ENDANGER *BANNER* AND THE OTHERS!

LOOK! A HELICOPTER IS MOVING IN OVER THE AMBULANCE!

HOW IN HOLY HANNAH DOES *IT* FIGURE IN *ALL* THIS?

I'VE GOT THE *CHLOROFORM* READY FOR BANNER!

GOOD! NOW IF I CAN JUST GET THE RHINO TO PULL HIM *ABOARD!*

HE'LL PROBABLY BE OFFENDED... THINK WE DIDN'T *TRUST* HIM TO PULL OFF THE ABDUCTION BY HIMSELF!

WHICH, COME TO THINK OF IT, WE *DIDN'T!*

BUT, BY THE *SAME TOKEN*, NEITHER DO THE SCIENTISTS EXPECT A *FRANTIC TEENAGER* TO APPEAR ON THE SCENE...

THERE'S THE AMBULANCE... RIGHT UP *AHEAD!* GOTTA REALLY *STEP* ON IT!

IT LOOKS LIKE SOME COSTUMED GUY IS PULLING BRUCE ---AND *BETTY ROSS* TOWARD THAT HOVER-ING HELICOPTER!

THAT *CHOPPER--*IT'S THE RHINO'S *GETAWAY* VEHICLE!

TRAIN YOUR *FIRE* ON IT-- *FAST!*

MY PARTNERS... MOTIONING FOR ME TO GET INTO THAT *'COPTER!*

THEY'RE GETTING AWAY WITH *BANNER!* STOP THEM! IN THE NAME OF REASON-- *STOP THEM!*

THEY'LL BE PROUD OF ME FOR THINKING TO BRING THE *GIRL* ALONG!

SHE MAY HELP THEM BE ABLE TO *CONTROL BANNER!*

9.

[70]

...THE HULK!

WHAT IS THIS...?

ONE MINUTE I'M HANGIN' ON TO A *SKINNY SCIENTIST*... AND THE *NEXT MINUTE*--!

BRUCE...NO! YOU MUSTN'T... YOU CAN'T...

HE'S TURNED INTO THE *HULK!* DROP HIM, YOU FOOL-- BEFORE IT'S *TOO LATE!*

YOU CAN'T HOLD THE *HULK* CAPTIVE!

YOU CONVINCED ME, BUDDY! I AIN'T EVEN GONNA *TRY!*

HAPPY LANDIN'S!

HOWEVER, AS THE GREAT GREEN GOLIATH BEGINS TO FALL, HE SUDDENLY *SEES*...

...*BETTY ROSS!*

SNAP!

SHE DOESN'T *WANT* TO BE WITH THESE MEN! HULK CAN *SENSE* IT!

MUST HANG ON WITH MY *LEG MUSCLES!* AND THEN ---

HAH! HULK DID PERFECT FLIP AND GRABBED HOLD WITH HIS *HAND!*

NOW I CAN *RESCUE* THE *GIRL!*

FIRST, I'LL BRING THE FLYING MACHINE TO THE *GROUND*...

BY STOPPING THESE *WHIRLING BLADES!*

RAKK!

THEN I GET GRIP *UNDER* THE PLANE...

...AND USE *MYSELF* TO CUSHION THE IMPACT WHEN WE HIT THE *GROUND!*

[71]

However, as the crippled aircraft hurtles toward the onrushing *Earth*...

SUDDENLY... EVERYTHING... *SPINNING*... FASTER AND... *FASTER!*

SUDDENLY... GETTING *DIZZY!*

HAVE TO STAY... *AWAKE!* CAN'T LET PLANE... *CRASH!*

Then, at that precise *MOMENT*...

GOING TO HIT HARD... *NOW!*

GETTING WEAKER EVERY *SECOND*... BUT SHIP IS *SAFE* NOW!

WHOOMP!

And that's more than we can say for a certain *Jolly Green Golem* just about now, as...

SO DIZZY... AND *CONFUSED!* CAN'T SEEM TO... *THINK* CLEARLY!

HEY... HE ACTS LIKE THERE'S SOMETHIN' *WRONG* WITH 'IM! AND THAT'S MY CUE TO *CHARGE!*

SUDDENLY...

HERE'S TO YER *HEALTH*, UGLY... AND HOPIN' I CAN MAKE IT A LOT *WORSE!*

:*AARRGGGHHHH!*

THAT'S IT, RHINO! BATTER HIM *SENSE-LESS*... WHILE I TAKE CARE OF HIS *LADY FRIEND!*

NO... YOU *CAN'T!* I DON'T CARE ABOUT *MYSELF*... BUT BRUCE... *THE HULK*... MUSTN'T BE *HARMED!*

SHUT UP AND *MOVE!*

YOU DON'T HAVE TO *WORRY* ABOUT IT, BOSS! HE'S SO DOPEY FROM THAT *CHLOROFORM* WE GAVE HIM...

...HE'S NO MORE OF A CHALLENGE TO ME THAN A *NORMAL MAN!*

I'LL FINISH 'IM AND BRING HIM BACK TO HEADQUARTERS IN *NO* TIME!

ALERT! ALERT! ALL AIRCRAFT BOUND FOR JFK WILL PROCEED TO *OTHER* AIRPORTS!

JFK IS *CLOSED* UNTIL FURTHER NOTICE! A STATE OF *EMERGENCY* EXISTS HERE!

ALL FAA OFFICIALS *TAKE COVER!* FOG AND SNOW-STORMS WE CAN HANDLE... BUT THE *HULK* AND THE *RHINO* ARE ANOTHER MATTER!

12

THEN, AS THE STEEL-SKINNED VILLAIN IS ABOUT TO DEAL A MIGHTY *DEATH BLOW*...

THWOP!

DIZZY SPELL HAS SUDDENLY *PASSED!*

NOW YOU'RE NOT FIGHTING A *SICK MAN* ANYMORE! NOW YOU MUST FACE... *THE HULK!*

AND YOU'RE TOO *PUNY*... TOO *AWKWARD* TO EVEN STAND A *CHANCE!*

NOW I HAVE TO FIND THE *GIRL!* DON'T KNOW *WHY*... BUT SOME *STRANGE*, UNCONTROLLABLE URGE TELLS ME... I *MUST!*

AND, AS THE OBSSESSED GREEN GARGOYLE LUMBERS THROUGH THE NUMEROUS GROUNDED *AIRCRAFT*...

STOP *STRUGGLING*, WOMAN! WE HAVE TO GET *AWAY* FROM HERE BEFORE...

NO... IT CAN'T BE! *STAY BACK*... OR I'LL *SHOOT!*

HULK-- STAY *BACK!!*

YOU THINK *BULLETS* CAN STOP THE HULK...

BRRAAKK!

... WHEN I CAN TEAR APART AN *AIRPLANE* WITH MY *BARE HANDS?*

LET ME *GO!* HE SEEMS TO *RECOGNIZE* ME! PERHAPS I CAN *REASON* WITH HIM!

PLEASE... IF YOU DON'T, HUNDREDS OF PEOPLE MAY BE *KILLED!*

YEAH... AND *ME* ALONG WITH THEM! YOU STAY IF YOU *WANT* TO! I'M *GOING!*

WHILE, A HUNDRED YARDS AWAY...

SO, THE COWARD'S *DESERTING ME!*

AND IF *HE'S* RUNNIN' OUT ... THERE AIN'T NO REASON WHY *I* SHOULD STICK AROUND AND GET MY *BRAINS* KICKED OUT!

13.

AND, AS THE *RHINO* TURNS TO FLEE...

IF...THERE'S ANY PART OF *BRUCE* WITHIN YOU, YOU'LL *LEAVE* HERE... AND NOT *HARM* ANYONE!

IF PEOPLE ARE *HURT*... THEY'LL HUNT YOU DOWN AND *KILL* YOU!

YOU'RE... *CONCERNED* FOR HULK? *WHY*?

BUT, IF YOU *CARE*... I MUST *PROTECT* YOU!

DON'T BE *AFRAID!* HULK WON'T *HURT* YOU!

I'LL PUT YOU HIGH ON *TOWER*... WHERE YOU'LL BE *SAFE!*

NOW...YOU WAIT *HERE!* HULK WILL COME *BACK* FOR YOU!

Y-YES! I... WILL!

I'M *TERRIFIED* OF HIM... AND YET, I FEEL CERTAIN I'VE NOTHING TO *FEAR* FROM HIM!

HULK HAS TO GO *FIGHT!* MUST PROVE TO THE WORLD THAT *NO ONE* IS STRONGER THAN THE *HULK!*

THEN, AFTER THE HULK HAS BOUNDED FAR ACROSS THE SPRAWLING AIRPORT IN BUT TWO *MIGHTY THOOMS*...

YOU! WHY DO YOU *RUN* FROM HULK! ARE YOU *AFRAID*?

HUH? THE *RHINO*... *SCARED*?

I JUST DIDN'T SEE THE *PERCENTAGE* IN SLUGGIN' IT OUT WITH YA!

BUT, SINCE YA PUT IT AS A MATTER'A *PRIDE*...

WOK!

IT WILL TAKE MORE THAN A BLOW LIKE A *FLYSWATTER* TO STOP THE *HULK!*

BUT ONE BLOW FROM *HULK* SHOULD BE PLENTY TO FINISH *YOU!*

14

THEN, SUMMONING ALL THE SUPERHUMAN *STRENGTH* WHICH SURGES THROUGH HIS POWERFUL BODY...

WSSSSH!

FOOOM!

...THE HULK SLAMS HIS FOE TO THE *PAVEMENT*...WITH ALL THE BRUTE FORCE OF A *THOUSAND PILE-DRIVERS!*

SEE! THE HULK WINS *AGAIN!* NOTHING... OR NO ONE CAN STOP ME!

GUESS AGAIN, CUDDLES! YOU AIN'T *TANGLIN'* WITH NO NUTHIN' OR NOBODY! YOU'RE UP AGAINST... *THE RHINO!*

WHAT'S THAT MEAN TO *ME?* IT TAKES MORE THAN A *NAME* AND A *COSTUME* TO MAKE YOU *MY EQUAL!*

BUT HULK WILL BE GLAD TO TEACH YOU THE *HARD WAY...* ...LIKE *THIS!*

WHRAM!

15

But, once *again* the rampaging rhino recovers, and...

If that's the best you can *dish out*...you better get ready to do some *takin'!*

Latch onta this...if yer able!

Hulk is *more* than able! But let's see if you can say the same for *yourself!*

I won't *have* to be! You're too *slow*...too *awkward* to hurl it back at me before I can...

That's it...come closer...*closer!*

NOW!

SMASH!

However, thinking only of a way to *defeat* his determined foe, the Hulk fails to notice that the truck is filled with highly explosive *jet fuel*, until...

WHOOSH!

--And both the gargantuan figures are instantaneously *consumed* by a blazing inferno of *liquid death*--!

16

But, the searing flames which would sizzle a normal man to a cinder in mere moments...does not spell the end for the *Hulk*, as...

AAAGGGHHHH! The fire's *blinding* me...can't *see*... can't get *out*!

Hulk must *escape*... but can't let the *Rhino* die *this* way!

Hulk will carry you to *safety*!

Then, we'll *continue* our fight--if you *can*!

Then, with a mighty flexing of his powerful legs, the Hulk springs high into the *air*...

...and, clinging tightly to his *unconscious adversary,* leaps into the cooling waters of *Jamaica Bay!*

Until, mere seconds which seem like an *eternity* later...

The danger's *over* now! Hulk has only a few *burns*!

But the fight's all *gone* from my foe! Hulk will leave him on the *shore!*

But, no sooner has the great green goliath *turned away,* than...

Runnin' from...a *fight,* huh? You still scared... I'll *beat* you?

Well...maybe I *understand!* 'cause I'm *human*...

...and not an *animal*...like you!

Hulk saved your *life*...and you still call him *names!* You still *challenge* Hulk?

Then, by the Hulk's hand you'll *die!*

17.

[77]

YER ALL *MOUTH*, GREENIE! YOU *TALK* A GOOD FIGHT...*BUT* WHEN THE CHIPS'RE DOWN, YOU AIN'T *NUTHIN'!*

BURNED...*BAD*, BUT GOTTA GET HIM TO...*FIGHT!*

NO! YOU'RE *TRYING* TO MAKE HULK MAD--BUT IT'S NO *USE!* YOU'RE HURT TOO BAD! HULK DOES NOT FIGHT A MAN WHO CAN'T EVEN *STAND!*

HE'S WALKIN' *OFF!* CAN'T LET HIM *DO* IT!

I'M HURT TOO BAD TO LIVE *ANYWAY!* THE LEAST I CAN DO IS...*DIE* A *WINNER!*

JUST GOT ENOUGH STRENGTH FOR ONE LAST...*CHARGE!*

GOTTA MAKE THIS ONE *COUNT*...OR I'LL NEVER GET ANOTHER...*CHANCE!*

;UUUNNNHHHH!;

I *DID* IT! NOW IF I CAN JUST HIT 'IM...*ONCE MORE* ...HE'LL BE *FINISHED!*

*B*UT, BEFORE THE HALF-CRAZED RHINO CAN *LAND HIS* BLOW...

YOU GOT BY WITH HITTING THE HULK FROM BEHIND *BEFORE*..BUT IT WON'T HAPPEN *AGAIN!*

TOO LATE! I'VE BLOWN... MY LAST *ROUND!*

SAY IT BEFORE YOU *DIE!* TELL ME THE WORDS YOU NEVER THOUGHT YOU'D *SAY...*

...NO ONE CAN *DEFEAT THE HULK!*

NEVER...NOT IN *THIS* LIFE... OR IN WHATEVER LIFE...I'M *GOIN'* TO!

18.

[78]

YER JUST LUCKY ...THAT *TRUCK* BLEW UP! OTHER-WISE... I'D HAVE WHIPPED YOU... *EASY!*

YOU *LIE!* HULK CAN'T BE BEAT BY *ANY MAN*... OR *ANYTHING!* SAY IT!

SAY IT OR I'LL...

...IT'S *NO USE!*

THE RHINO IS...*DEAD!*

BUT *I* KNOW I WOULD HAVE BEATEN HIM!

AND THE *REST* OF THE WORLD WILL KNOW IT, TOO!

HOWEVER, AT THAT MOMENT, ON THE VERY SPOT WHERE THE HULK LEFT *BETTY ROSS*...

SHE'S ONLY *FAINTED!* SHE'LL BE *ALL RIGHT!*

HURRY UP AND GET HER *DOWN* FROM HERE BEFORE.. *LOOK!* OVER *THERE--!*

HERE COMES... THE HULK!

THEN, WITHIN SECONDS, AS THE RESCUE WORKERS REACH *STREET LEVEL*...

WHERE'S THE *GIRL?* WHY DIDN'T SHE *WAIT* FOR HULK? I *TOLD* HER I'D...

THERE SHE IS ...WITH GENERAL WHO'S ALWAYS *HUNTING* ME!

GIVE GIRL *BACK*... OR HULK WILL KILL YOU *ALL!* SEND HER TO ME *NOW!*

OVER MY *BODY*, YOU *MURDERER!* YOU'LL NEVER *TOUCH* HER AGAIN!

I SWEAR YOU'LL NEVER *LIVE* TO!

THREATS DON'T SCARE *HULK!* I'LL GET THE GIRL ONE WAY OR THE *OTHER!*

UNLESS I HEAR *HER* SAY THAT... SHE *HATES* HULK!

19.

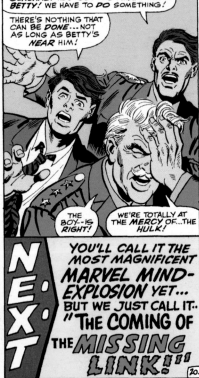

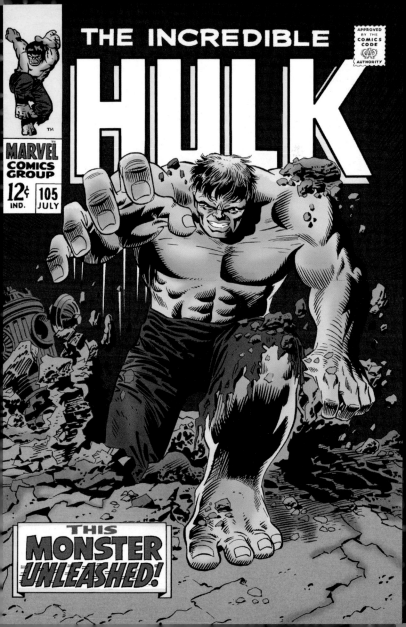

THERE'S NO WAY I CAN *ESCAPE* HIM NOW... WITHOUT FALLING TO MY *DEATH!*

BUT, DO I REALLY *WANT* TO ESCAPE... AS LONG AS THERE'S A CHANCE OF *SAVING* HIM FROM HIMSELF...?

WAIT! I HAVE AN IDEA! PERHAPS...

HULK... TAKE ME TO MY *HOTEL!*

IF I'M GOING *WITH* YOU, I'LL NEED A CHANGE OF *CLOTHES*... *MONEY...!*

GIRL NEEDS *NOTHING...* NOT WHEN SHE'S WITH *HULK!*

BUT, HULK WILL DO AS GIRL *WISHES!*

THEN, SHE WON'T BE *AFRAID* ANY MORE!

AND, SCANT MOMENTS LATER...

WE'RE *HERE!* BUT, HULK DOESN'T *LIKE* BEING IN CITY!

WE'LL ONLY BE HERE FOR A *FEW MINUTES!*

WAIT IN THIS *ALLEY* ...TILL I *RETURN!*

GARAGE ENTRANCE

AND, ABOVE ALL, DON'T *DO* ANYTHING... OR *HARM* ANYONE!

BUT, EVEN AS THE DISTRAUGHT GIRL RUSHES THRU THE DARKENED *GARAGE,* HOPING TO TELEPHONE HER FATHER, GENERAL ROSS...

HOTEL GARAGE

HOLD IT, AL! SOUNDS LIKE SOMEBODY COMIN'!

THAT'S ALL WE *NEED* ...A CRUMMY *WITNESS!*

KLIK! KLIK!

WHO-EVER IT IS... *GRAB* 'IM!

WE CAN ALWAYS USE A *HOSTAGE!*

HEY, LOOK... IT'S A *CHICK!*

SORRY, BABY, BUT WE PLANNED THIS CAR-HEIST 'CAUSE THE *HULK* HAD EVERYBODY SCARED OFF THE *STREETS...*

AND, YOU AIN'T ABOUT TO *SPOIL* IT!

:MMMMFF...!:

MUFFLE 'ER! DON'T LET HER *SCREAM!*

NO! DON'T *TOUCH* GIRL... OR HULK WILL CRUSH YOU TO A *PULP!*

IT...IT'S *HIM* ...THE *HULK!!*

WE NEVER DREAMED... HE'D SHOW UP *HERE!*

STAY BACK! WE DIDN'T *MEAN* NUTHIN'!... HONEST!

2

QUICKLY, HER MIND ONLY TOO FAMILIAR WITH HER RESCUER'S *STEAM-ROLLER POWER,* BETTY ATTEMPTS TO *STAY* THE GREEN BEHEMOTH...

BRUCE...HULK...FOR THE LOVE OF HEAVEN, *STOP!*

IF..IF YOU HARM THEM, THE ARMY WILL *NEVER* LET YOU ALONE!

HULK DOESN'T *CARE!* JUST KNOW THEY TRIED TO *HURT* GIRL!

KEE--RAKK!

FOR *THAT...* THEY MUST *PAY!!*

RUN FOR IT, AL! *MOVE!*

YA THINK I NEED A BLASTED *BOOK OF INSTRUCTIONS?*

STAND *CLEAR,* FEMALE...

...WHILE HULK *SMASHES* THOSE WHO FLEE HIM!

I CAN'T *STAND* ANY *MORE!*

I LOVE *BRUCE BANNER*...BUT NOT...*THIS MONSTER..!*

MONSTER? SHE CALLED THE HULK...A *MONSTER!?*

BUT...HULK JUST WANTS TO *HELP* HER..!

WAIT! SOMETHING'S *HAPPENING...*

HULK'S *CHANGING...* TURNING BACK TO *BRUCE BANNER!*

BUT...DON'T *WANT* TO BECOME HUMAN! *DON'T WANT TO...!*

I DON'T *BLAME* YA, CREEP...'CAUSE EVERYBODY KNOWS THAT BANNER'S JUST ANOTHER *EGGHEAD!*

AN' THAT MEANS MY *GUN* AIN'T USELESS ANY MORE!

BRAK!

KNOCK IT OFF, *ROCKY*...AND *BLOW!*

UNNHHH!

I'M *HIT*...JUST AS I FINISHED *CHANGING!*

BUT...I CAN'T *DIE!* NOT *NOW*...NOT LIKE *THIS*...!!

3.

THEN, THE BULLET RIPPING THRU HIS NOW-VULNERABLE FLESH, THE STRICKEN SCIENTIST **COLLAPSES** AT BETTY ROSS'S FEET...

HOW COULD THE HULK HAVE BECOME **BRUCE** AGAIN---FOR NO APPARENT **REASON?**

AND...WHY DID IT HAVE TO HAPPEN...AT THE **WORST** POSSIBLE MOMENT?

OH, BRUCE... **BRUCE**...

BUT NOW, WE MUST TEMPORARILY **LEAVE** THIS EMOTION-DRENCHED SCENE, AND VIEW A MYSTERIOUS FOREIGN **FREIGHTER**, AS IT SKIRTS THE HARBORS OF **NEW YORK**...

THE **X-CAPSULE** HAS BEEN **FIRED**, COMRADE!

OUR MISSION IS **COMPLETE!**

WHOOSH!

BUT, MY FRIEND, I HAVE NOT BEEN INFORMED WHAT THE CAPSULE **CONTAINS!**

IS IT SET TO **EXPLODE** UPON CONTACT?

FOOL! THAT IS WHY YOU WERE NOT ENTRUSTED WITH OUR **SECRET PURPOSE**... YOU THINK ONLY IN TERMS OF TELLTALE **BOMBS!**

LOOK OUT THIS **PORTHOLE!**

WHILE **SEARCHLIGHTS** PROBE THE SKIES FOR THE INFAMOUS **HULK**, WE HAVE CHOSEN THIS TIME TO **STRIKE!**

AND, STRIKE WE **SHALL**...DIRECTLY AT THE AREA KNOWN AS **WALL STREET!**

BUT HOW..?

BY NOW, THE JUST-FIRED **X-CAPSULE** HAS BEEN GUIDED TO A **SOFT LANDING** AGAINST THE DOCK...

...WHERE IT WILL AUTOMATICALLY **OPEN**...

WHOMP!

AND, WHILE WE CONVERSE, IT IS NOW **SINKING**... BUT NOT BEFORE IT HAS DIVULGED ITS MIND-STAGGERING **CARGO**...

A CARGO WHICH **LIVES**... WHICH **BREATHES**...

...AND WHICH EVEN NOW DOUBTLESS TREADS THE **ROTTING PLANKS** OF THE DARKENED WHARF...!

4

"NOT LONG AGO, OUR ACCURSED *EASTERN ALLIES* CONDUCTED A TOP-SECRET *ATOMIC TEST*...THE FORCE OF WHICH WAS DIRECTED MOSTLY *UNDERGROUND*..."

"BUT, DUE TO FAULTY CALCULATIONS, THE EXPLOSION CAUSED A SEVERE *INTERNAL UPHEAVAL*...AS MOLTEN LAVA SCATTERED *RADIOACTIVE ORE* IN ALL DIRECTIONS..."

KA-VOOOM!

"ONLY A FEW DAYS LATER, A WANDERING *NOMAD* CAME UPON A HALF-HUMAN, HALF-BESTIAL *FORM*... CRAWLING DAZEDLY OUT OF A *FISSURE* ON THE NORTHERN EDGE OF THE TEST AREA---"

"THE UNFORTUNATE NOMAD *DIED* A FEW DAYS LATER... OF *RADIATION EXPOSURE*..."

"MEANWHILE, A TEAM OF *MILITARY SCIENTISTS* WAS SENT OUT TO CAPTURE THE BRUTE...WHICH APPARENTLY HAD SURVIVED IN *SUSPENDED ANIMATION* FOR COUNTLESS AGES, TO BE REVIVED BY THE BLAST..."

THERE HE IS!

IT'S *UNBELIEVABLE!* EVOLUTION'S *MISSING LINK*...ALIVE!

AND, WE MUST *KEEP* HIM THAT WAY! FIRE YOUR *GAS PELLETS!*

RRRRH...

"SOON, SUBJECTED TO A SERIES OF TESTS, THE SEMI-HUMAN CREATURE BEGAN TO *CHANGE* IN APPEARANCE...TO THE *AMAZEMENT* OF THE SCIENTISTS..."

LOOK! THE APELIKE *HAIR* WHICH COVERED HIS BODY...IT'S *FALLING OUT!*

AND...WHAT ARE THOSE WEIRD *CRYSTALS* APPEARING ON HIM?

5.

"BUT, SECONDS LATER, AS THE CURIOUS SCIENTISTS MOVED IN TO EXAMINE HIM MORE CLOSELY, HE SUDDENLY *SPRANG UPWARD*..."

HE'S RIPPING HIS *BONDS*... AS IF THEY WERE *PAPER!*

IT..IT *CAN'T* BE! HE WAS *HALF DEAD*...UNABLE EVEN TO *STAND*...!

RRRMMF!

"AND THEN, BEFORE THEIR AMAZED EYES, HE SEEMED SUDDENLY *TRANSFORMED* BY THE NAMELESS CRYSTALS INTO A GLOWING, PULSATING ENGINE OF *DESTRUCTION*.."

"NO LONGER WAS HE A PRIMITIVE *MISSING LINK*... BUT A *RADIO-ACTIVE MONSTER*, SUCH AS HAD NEVER BEFORE WALKED THE EARTH..."

"FEARFUL FOR THEIR OWN SAFETY, THE MEN OF SCIENCE *FIRED* UPON IT... BUT TO *NO AVAIL*..."

NOTHING *STOPS* THE *BEAST-MAN!*

WE CAN *STUN* HIM...BUT ONLY FOR A *MOMENT!*

KRAK! KRAK!

"THEY EVEN CALLED IN *TROOPS*...WITH *LIGHT MORTARS*..."

FWHOOM!

"YET, THIS MERELY *INFURIATED* THE BEAST-MAN...SO THAT HE LASHED OUT AGAINST THEM WITH THE RAGE OF A MADDENED *DREADNOUGHT*..."

SMASH!

"FINALLY, HE WAS *SUBDUED*...BY MEANS OF A GREAT BOMBARDMENT OF *SLEEPING GAS*... AND, WITHIN HOURS, MILITARY OFFICIALS MADE A *TOP-LEVEL DECISION*..."

OUR SCIENTISTS PREDICT THAT, WHEN HE *AWAKENS* ONLY DAYS FROM NOW, EVEN *GAS PELLETS* WILL NO LONGER STOP HIM!

HE MUST BE *DISPOSED* OF SOMEHOW... AND, I HAVE A *PLAN!*

THEN *SPEAK*, COMRADE! IN THE NAME OF MAO... *SPEAK!*

"AND SO, AN INGENIOUS *PLAN* WAS BORN! WHILE STILL UNCONSCIOUS, THE DANGEROUSLY RADIO-ACTIVE MONSTER WAS PUT INTO A LEAD-LINED *CAPSULE*... AND PUT ABOARD THE FREIGHTER OF A *SATELLITE NATION*..."

WHEN HE AWAKENS, HE WILL BE IN THE DECADENT *UNITED STATES!*

HE WILL WREAK *HAVOC* AND *DESTRUCTION*... AKIN TO NOTHING THE WORLD HAS EVER *SEEN!*

6.

AND NOW LET'S RETURN TO THE PULSE-POUNDING *PRESENT*...

...AS THE CRYSTALLINE MONSTER, FREED FROM THE X-CAPSULE, ROAMS THE NEARLY DESERTED STREETS OF DARKENED, DOWNTOWN *NEW YORK*...

WALSTON WAREHOUSE

HOW... DID I *GET* HERE?

NOT *KNOW*... THIS PLACE!

STORAGE

NOT *LIKE*... THIS *PLACE*!*

*OF *COURSE* WE'RE TRANS-LATING OUR GUTTERAL GARGOYLE'S GROWLINGS FOR YOU! WE COULDN'T HAVE IT SAID OUR LINGUISTIC-MINDED BULLPEN COULDN'T DECIPHER *MISSING-LINK DIALECT*!
--- SAVE-A-FACE STAN.

MEANWHILE, A DESPERATE *BETTY ROSS* HAS MANAGED TO GET THE WOUNDED *BRUCE BANNER* TO HER CAR, INSIDE THE HOTEL GARAGE ---

BRUCE...YOU'RE *ALIVE*!

I WAS SO AFRAID... THOSE WOULD-BE CAR THIEVES HAD *KILLED* YOU...!

IT'S ONLY... A *FLESH WOUND*... I THINK!

..THOUGH THAT'S NOT STOPPING IT FROM *HURTING*!

EXIT

BUT, WHERE..?

NO TIME FOR *QUESTIONS* NOW, MY DARLING!

I'VE GOT TO GET YOU TO A *DOCTOR*!

BUT, WHEN IT *RAINS*, IT *POURS*... AND SO, AS BETTY'S CAR *CAREENS* INTO THE STREET---

YOU THERE... *HOLD IT*!

PULL OVER! WE WANT TO *TALK* TO YOU...

...ABOUT THE *SHOOTING* WE JUST *HEARD*!

POLICE

NO! DON'T STOP FOR *ANYTHING*, BETTY!

STEP ON IT... *FAST*!

YES, BRUCE! I... I SUPPOSE I *MUST*!

IF THEY STOP US *NOW*, THEY'LL TAKE *BRUCE*... BECAUSE THEY'LL KNOW HE'S THE *HULK*!

7.

THEN, AS THE FLEEING CAR HURTLES OFF INTO THE *NIGHT*...

LOOK...IN THE *MIRROR!* THEY'RE *FOLLOWING* US!

I'M DRIVING AS FAST AS I *DARE*, BRUCE!

BUT, THEY'RE *BOUND* TO CATCH US, ANYWAY!

FASTER, BETTY... *FASTER!!*

NO! THEY *MUSTN'T!*

I WON'T BE *CAGED*... LIKE SOME *MADDENED BEAST!*

WAIT! ...THE *EXCITEMENT*... MY *PULSE!*

IT'S *RACING*... CHANGING ME *AGAIN*...!

BRUCE...WHAT ARE YOU...??

SLOW DOWN.. AT THE NEXT *CORNER*..!

DON'T WANT YOU... *MIXED* UP IN THIS...!

YET, INSTANTS LATER, THE FIGURE THAT TUMBLES FROM THE SPEEDING VEHICLE IS *NOT* THAT OF A *WEAKENED SCIENTIST*...

...BUT THAT OF THE *GARGANTUAN*, GREEN-SKINNED *HULK!!*

THE *HULK* CAN TAKE CARE OF *HIMSELF!*

NO NEED FOR THE *GIRL*...TO BE IN DANGER!

IF ONLY I CAN FIND *DADDY!*

MAYBE HE CAN *HELP* BRUCE..BEFORE IT'S *TOO LATE!*

EVERYBODY *LOOKING* FOR THE HULK...EVERY-BODY OUT TO *GET* HIM!

BUT, *NOBODY* CATCHES THE HULK! *NOBODY!*

ONE GIANT *LEAP*, AND...

HULK *CAN'T* JUMP...NOT ENOUGH *STRENGTH!*

DON'T KNOW *WHY*... BUT SOMETHING IS WRONG WITH *LEG!*

MUST FIND *ANOTHER* WAY OUT OF HERE!

THUS, UNABLE TO RECALL THE *WOUND* HE RE-CEIVED AS BANNER, THE HULK IS BEWILDERED... CONFUSED...

8

BUT, IF OUR HARASSED HERO'S *MEMORY* MOMENTARILY FAILS HIM---HIS SENSES STAGGERING *MIGHT* DEFINITELY DOES *NOT*..!

HOLY HANNAH! HE'S KNOCKIN' A HOLE---THRU SOLID *CONCRETE!*

THE HULK *ALWAYS* FINDS A WAY...

IF HE CAN'T GO *UP*...

T-H WOMP!

UNNHHH! THAT KNOCKED THE *BREATH*--- OUT OF HULK!

STILL, THE HULK IS LUCKY---TO LAND ON TOP OF *SUBWAY TRAIN!*

IT WILL CARRY HIM AWAY--- *FAR* AWAY---

T-HUD!

...WHERE NO ONE *LOOKS* FOR HIM!

N BROADWAY EXPRESS
57 STREET
CONEY IS.

NOW WHAT'S HAPPENING TO THIS BLASTED SUBWAY?

AFTER ALL THE *TAXES* WE PAY...

...HE'LL GO *DOWN!*

N CONEY IS

JUST THEN, EVEN AS THE ONRUSHING TRAIN CARRIES ITS GROTESQUE PASSENGER AWAY FROM HIS PURSUERS, *ANOTHER* THOUGHT SUDDENLY DAWNS IN HIS SOMEWHAT CLOUDED CRANIUM...

WAIT!! WHY IS THE HULK *RUNNING*... LIKE SOME PUNY *HUMAN?*

THE HULK RUNS FROM *NOTHING* ON *EARTH!*

MUST *STAY*... AND *FIGHT!*

WHOMM!

9.

THE NEXT INSTANT, DESPITE THE TEMPORARY WEAKNESS IN HIS COLOSSAL LEGS, THE GREEN GOLIATH *SMASHES* UPWARD, HIS MASSIVE FIST SHATTERING SOOTED STEEL AND TILE...

KRUNCH!

HULK *PANICKED*... TRIED TO FLEE, LIKE FRIGHTENED *RAT!*

BUT, HE WILL RUN *NO MORE!*

N BROADWAY

FOR, *NOBODY* IS STRONGER THAN THE *HULK!*

AND, *NOTHING* CAN STOP THE HULK... WHEN HE'S *ANGRY*...

GRAKK!

NOTHING!!

SKRAK

BUT, AS SHEER, STARK *COINCIDENCE* WOULD HAVE IT, THE HULK HAS CHOSEN TO SURFACE AT PERHAPS THE *ONLY* PLACE WHERE STANDS ONE WHO *CAN* STOP THE HULK...

...FOR, AS THE WOUNDED BEHEMOTH *EMERGES* INTO THE DARKENED CITY...

RRRRR

WHAT IS *THAT?* SOME HUGE *MONSTER*...

IS *IT* AFTER HULK ---LIKE EVERYBODY *ELSE?*

WHAT DOES IT *WANT* FROM THE HULK?

10.

WITHOUT WARNING, THE SAVAGELY AWESOME TITAN *WHIRLS*...LASHING OUT WITH THE FURY OF A ROARING *MAELSTROM*...

NOT LIKE... THIS *PLACE*!

NOT LIKE *CREATURES* I FOUND HERE... WILL *KILL*!

UNNNHH!

WHOMPP!

BEAST-MAN HIT THE HULK WITH POWER OF A *PILEDRIVER*!

FEEL *STRANGE*. IT *BURNS* WHERE HE HIT ME..BURNS LIKE *FIRE*!

NO ONE *HURTS* THE HULK...AND *LIVES*!!

HE GIVES OFF SOME KIND OF *RADIATION*...BUT THE *HULK* ISN'T AFRAID!

HULK WAS *CREATED* BY RADIATION!

NOW IT TURNS ITS *BACK*...

KRRRAK!

...AS IF HULK NOT WORTHY OF ITS *NOTICE*!

HULK WILL SHOW THE BEAST-MAN!

...SHOW HIM WHO IS THE *STRONGEST* OF ALL!

RRRAAKK

NOW, HULK WILL ROLL WHOLE *STREET* OVER THE MONSTER...

...LIKE CONCRETE, *CARPET*!

BRRRONCHH!

:AGHRRR!:

BUT THEN, TO THE GREEN GOLEM'S SHEER *AMAZEMENT*, HIS UNEARTHLY PREY ABRUPTLY EMITS AN OVER-POWERING *RADIOACTIVE AURA...*

FIZZZTTT

BLINDLY, INSTINCTIVELY, IT *BURNS THRU* THE CRUSHING RUBBLE WITH THE DEVASTATING HEAT OF A MINIATURE *SUN...*

NOW... I AM *FREE* AGAIN!

FREE TO SMASH THE *GREEN CREATURE* THAT THREATENS ME!

HULK DOES NOT *BELIEVE* IT!

IT MELTED THE CONCRETE... LIKE *BUTTER!*

AND NOW, IT COMES AFTER...THE *HULK!*

THUS, A MOMENT LATER, TWO UNBELIEVABLY POWERFUL *JUGGERNAUTS* CLASHED IN CLOSE COMBAT...EACH THINKING THAT THE OTHER ORIGINALLY *ATTACKED* IT...

THEN, *SUDDENLY...*

FIST... SHATTERS PART OF BEAST-MAN'S SHOULDER ...INTO *CRYSTALS!*

BUT...THE *BURNING* HURTS HULK...WORSE THAN HIS *VICTIM!*

HAH! HE IS *STARTLED...* CONFUSED!

THUMP!

I MUST *STRIKE...* NOW!!

AND, EVEN AS THE CRYSTALLINE CELLS OF THE BEAST-MAN'S BODY *FUSE TOGETHER* AGAIN, THRU THE POWER OF *RADIATION...*

AAARRHH! MY ENEMY HAS THE HULK...IN A *BEAR-HUG!*

HULK *BURNS...* BURNS ALL OVER!!

KRUNNCH!

MUST *CRUSH* MY ATTACKER... ONCE AND FOR ALL!

12.

Panel 1: HULK FEELS *WEAK*... BUT STILL CAN *PROTECT* HIMSELF!

WHONNK!

GREEN ENEMY... WILL SOON *MELT* IN HEAT!

HE CAN'T FIGHT... MUCH *LONGER!*

Panel 2: SUDDENLY... *NO!* THE HULK... IS *BURNING UP.* GETTING WEAKER...!

SOON! SQUEEZE *TIGHTER*... MY ENEMY WILL *DIE!*

Panel 3: AND, AS THE ALL-CONSUMING *RADIATION* FROM THE *BEAST-MAN* MIXES WITH THE *GAMMA RAYS* FROM THE HULK'S OWN BODY...

...ONCE AGAIN THE MYSTICAL *TRANS-FORMATION* BEGINS...

BUT, *THIS* TIME, WITH A *DIFFER-ENCE...!*

Panel 4: *PUZZLED,* CONFUSED, THE PRIMITIVE CREATURE *DROPS* HIS UNRECOGNIZABLE VICTIM...THE LIMP FORM OF A *NUCLEAR SCIENTIST*...

THIS IS NOT... *GREEN* ONE WHO *ATTACKED* ME!

PINK-SKINNED ONE... *NOT WORTHY* OF BATTLE!

UHNNN!

Panel 5: *THEN,* DISDAINFULLY, THE AWESOME ANTHROPOID STALKS AWAY...

..EVEN AS STRANGE, UNFAMILIAR *WORDS* FLOW FROM THE TONGUE OF *BRUCE BANNER*...

HULK *BEATEN...* BECAUSE HE SUDDENLY CHANGED TO THIS *SHAPE!*

WHERE DID IT *COME FROM?*

MUST GET BACK MY *OWN* BODY... SO I CAN GET *REVENGE!*

Panel 6: *YES,* IT'S *TRUE*...THE BRAIN OF THE BESTIAL *HULK* IS NOW IMPRISONED IN THE WOUNDED FORM OF *BRUCE BANNER*...AND, WHILE YOU DIGEST *THAT* LITTLE PIECE OF NEWS...

JUST KEEP THE PUBLIC OFF THE STREETS... AND THE *ARMY* WILL TAKE CARE OF THE *HULK!*

EVEN NOW, A *SECRET DEVICE* IS BEING *FASHIONED...*

...WHICH WILL *ELIMINATE* THAT *MONSTROUS* MENACE... *FOREVER!*

13

"... A DEVICE BEING DEVELOPED BY THE ONE AND ONLY *REED RICHARDS*, FROM NOTES WRITTEN BY *BANNER* HIMSELF, SEVERAL MONTHS AGO..."

YES, SIR...HE'S PUTTING THE *FINAL TOUCHES* ON IT NOW!

YOU MEAN I JUST *PUT* THEM, YOUNGSTER!

YOU'D BETTER TAKE IT *FAST*...BEFORE I CHANGE MY MIND AND *DESTROY* IT!

THEN...HIS VOICE SOLEMN, HIS MANNER STERN ...THE LEADER OF THE FABULOUS F.F. *TURNS*...

JUST REMEMBER...IF IT FINISHES THE *HULK*, IT MAY ALSO KILL *BRUCE BANNER!*

IF HE HADN'T DESIGNED THE PLANS *HIMSELF* FOR JUST SUCH AN EMERGENCY... I'D NEVER HAVE *BUILT* IT!

MAYBE...WE SHOULDN'T GO *THRU* WITH IT, MAJOR TALBOT! MAYBE THE HULK CAN BE STOPPED SOME *OTHER* WAY...!

YOU KNOW *BETTER*, SON... AND SO, IN HIS OWN WAY, DID *BANNER!*

THE HULK *MUST* BE DESTROYED --- NO MATTER *WHAT!*

BUT, IF *BANNER* DIES WHEN THE HULK DOES... *BETTY* WILL NEVER FORGIVE ME!

THE QUESTION IS... WILL I FORGIVE MY-SELF?

MR. RICHARDS... CAN'T YOU...?

I'VE DONE... ALL I CAN, SON!

FROM HERE ON, IT'S UP TO THE ARMY, AND MAJOR TALBOT!

MEANWHILE, *POLICE*...INVESTIGATING THE REPORT OF A VIOLENT *DISTURBANCE* IN DOWNTOWN *MANHATTAN*...ARE MAKING A STARTLING *DISCOVERY*...

PETE...*LOOK*... OVER THERE... COMING OUT OF THAT *ALLEY!*

IT...IT'S NOT *POSSIBLE!*

JUST THEN, THE GLARING SPOTLIGHT *OUTLINES* THE GLOWING FIGURE OF THE CRYSTALLINE CREATURE...

AND WORSE... IT *ENRAGES* HIM...

AHHHRRR! MORE HUMANS COME...PUNY PINK ONES!

I WILL SMASH THEM...!

GOLDSMIT

14

HOLY HANNAH! HE GLOWS LIKE A NEON LIGHT!

STOP! HALT, OR I'LL SHOOT!

HA! PINK ONE FIRES...PEBBLES!

KRACKK!

WH..? EVEN BULLETS DON'T STOP HIM!

AND NOW...IT KNOCKED THE GUN OUT OF MY HAND--WITH A SINGLE SWEEP--!

NOTHING... STAND IN WAY! NOT LIKE...PUNY PEOPLE!

NOT LIKE BRIGHT LIGHT!

KRASH!

NOT FAR AWAY, THE SLIGHT FIGURE OF DR. BRUCE BANNER HAS PULLED HIMSELF TO HIS FEET, JUST AS...

HULK IS GETTING OWN BODY BACK ...CHANGING AGAIN!

MUST FIND STRANGE MONSTER!

NOW HULK IS HIMSELF AGAIN! NO ONE MAKE FOOL OF THE HULK--NOT EVEN...

HAH! THERE HE IS NOW...FIGHTING POLICE!

THE HULK HAVE NO LOVE FOR POLICE... BUT NOT HAVE LOVE FOR GLOWING GIANT, EITHER!

HULK FINISH THIS FIGHT!

ONCE MORE, THE IMPACT OF THE HULK'S PILEDRIVER FIST SHATTERS THE CRYSTALLINE ARMOR OF THE RADIO- ACTIVE CREATURE...BUT THIS TIME...

...THIS TIME, HULK WAS CAREFUL ...DIDN'T GET IN MONSTER'S CLUTCHES!

POW!

15

THE HULK IS *STRONGER* THAN MONSTER! IT SHATTERS...

...SPLINTERS INTO *GLASSY PIECES*... LIKE *BEFORE!*

FZZZZT!

HULK DOESN'T UNDERSTAND WHY THE MONSTER TRIES TO *DESTROY* EVERYTHING...

BUT *NO ONE* DESTROYS THE *HULK!*

MORE *POLICE* COME!

HULK *READY* FOR THEM!

O LEARY ...*LOOK!* HELP'S COMING!

TAKING ADVANTAGE OF HIS FOE'S TEMPORARY IMMOBILITY, THE *GREEN GOLIATH* TURNS HIS GREAT POWER ON THE APPROACHING POLICE REINFORCEMENTS ---

SKREEEEEE

POLICE NOT INTERFERE WITH HULK'S *PRIVATE FIGHT!* HULK HANDLE BEAST-MAN BY *HIMSELF!*

THE SLIGHT RESPITE, HOWEVER, ALLOWS JUST ENOUGH TIME FOR ITS GLOWING *HEAT* TO WELD THE RADIOACTIVE TITAN'S CRYSTAL COMPONENTS TOGETHER...

CAR TAKE HURT POLICEMAN TO *HOSPITAL!*

NOW THE *HULK* WILL TAKE CARE OF *MONSTER!*

AGHRRRR

16

MUST FIX IT... SO THE MONSTER NEVER *GETS UP* AGAIN!

JUST *STRENGTH* ENOUGH LEFT... IN HURT *LEG*... TO LEAP UP SIDE OF *BUILDING*... ...AND *SMASH* IT!

INSTANTLY, JUST AS A SPEEDING CAR SCREECHES TO A HALT IN THE SHADOWS, A TORRENT OF *RUBBLE* CRASHES TO THE STREET BELOW...

MAJOR TALBOT! *LOOK*... UP THERE! THE *HULK!*

WATCH *OUT!* THE WHOLE SIDE OF THE BUILDING'S COMING DOWN!

KA-

POW!

I'LL *BURY* THE MONSTER UNDER *CONCRETE*... BRICKS... *STEEL!*

HE'S ON A RAMPAGE, ALL RIGHT... JUST LIKE THEY SAID! LET ME GET A *SHOT* AT HIM WITH THIS MACHINE RICHARDS RIGGED UP!

NO... *WAIT!* WE'VE GOT TO FIND OUT WHAT HAPPENED TO *BETTY*, FIRST.

HULK! *HULK!* CAN YOU *HEAR* ME?

IT'S THE BOY... *RICK*.. WITH ARMY FRIEND OF GIRL!

THE *FOOLS!* DON'T THEY KNOW WHAT LIES BENEATH THAT PILE OF *BRICKS?*

HULK NOT *FINISHED* WITH BURNING *BEAST-MAN* YET!

ANSWER ME! WHERE'S THE *GIRL?* WHAT HAVE YOU *DONE* WITH HER?

18

BUT, EVEN AS THE MIGHTY BEHEMOTH SEIZES AND CRUSHES THE FRAGILE MACHINE IN HIS VISE-LIKE HANDS, A *STRANGE*, YET ALL-TOO-*FAMILIAR*, FEELING POSSESSES HIS MASSIVE BODY...

HULK WILL *DESTROY!*

HULK... ≡UHNNN!≡

FEEL *CHANGE* COMING AGAIN!

HULK'S SKIN IS GETTING *PALE*... I'M TURNING BACK TO *BRUCE BRANNER!*

I.. I *AM* BRUCE BANNER! AND MY HAND...

BUT... WHY? WHY??

...IT'S *BURNED*, FROM TRYING TO HOLD THAT MONSTROUS OGRE..!

JUST THEN, EVEN AS BRUCE'S THOUGHTS FOCUS ON THE IMMINENT *DANGER*...

AHRRRRRRR!

WHROOOOM!

L-LOOK! WHAT ON EARTH IS *THAT?* --RISING OUT OF THE *DEBRIS?*

THAT'S WHAT THE *HULK*..WAS TRYING TO *WARN* YOU ABOUT!

IT'S SOME SORT OF *RADIOACTIVE* MONSTER!

RUN FOR IT, YOU TWO! GET OUT OF HERE! I'LL....

NO, MAJOR! MERE *BULLETS* WON'T STOP HIM! AND... IT'S *ME* HE'S AFTER!

IF ONLY... IF ONLY I WERE THE *HULK* AGAIN!

YET SOMEHOW HE *RECOGNIZES* ME...HE'S COMING FOR ME..!

RUN, I TELL YOU! RUN!!

NO MATTER *WHAT* HAPPENS, BRUCE, WE CAN'T LEAVE YOU HERE TO *DIE...ALONE!!*

WOULD'JA BELIEVE... TO BE HULKINUED?

20.

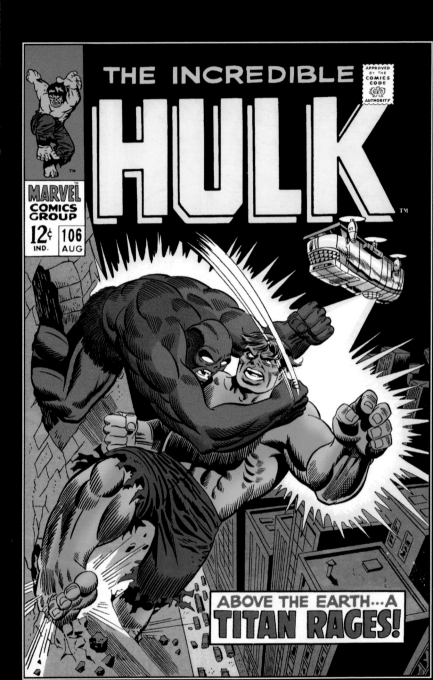

PONDEROUSLY, INEVITABLY, THE BEAST-MAN LUMBERS EVER NEARER, *RADIATION-DRENCHED HANDS* LASHING OUT AT THE HELPLESS TRIO BEFORE HIM...

GREEN-SKINNED FOE HAS *CHANGED* ...BUT DOES NOT *FOOL* ME...

I WILL *GET* HIM, *KILL* HIM... EVEN IF I MUST ALSO SMASH *OTHER* PUNY PINK ONES!*

*THIS, OF COURSE, IS BUT A *LOOSE TRANS-LATION* OF THE ORIGINAL *MISSING LINK* LANGUAGE --STIPU-LATIN' STAN.

AT THAT INSTANT, WITH THE WHINING ROAR OF AN *EVER-ACCELERATING ENGINE,* BETTY'S CAR HURTLES ONTO THE SCENE...

IT'S *BRUCE!* HE'S NO LONGER THE *HULK!*

BUT THAT *THING*... THAT *NIGHTMARE MONSTER*...IT'S ABOUT TO STRIKE HIM AND THE OTHERS!

IF I *HESITATE,* THEY'LL ALL *DIE*...THERE'S ONLY *ONE THING* TO DO--

AND BEING EVERY INCH THE DAUGHTER OF *THUNDERBOLT ROSS,* BETTY *DOES* IT--!

WHLAM!

NO!

GOOD LORD!

THAT CAR... IT'S *BETTY'S!*

WHAT HAS SHE *DONE??*

THEN, THE SHATTERING *IMPACT* FADES INTO DEADLY *SILENCE*...

SHE WAS THROWN *CLEAR,* BUT... *TALBOT!* IS SHE... SHE...?

I DON'T *KNOW,* MAN, I DON'T *KNOW!*

3

MERCIFULLY *UNAWARE* OF HIS DAUGHTER'S FATE, *GENERAL ROSS* CONTINUES COORDINATING THE CAMPAIGN AGAINST THE *HULK...*

I'VE HAD *NO WORD* FROM MAJOR TALBOT ON WHETHER OR NOT REED RICHARDS' WEAPON *WORKED*, FURY...

THEN IT'S *MY BALL*, RIGHT?

DON'T THINK I *LIKE* PUTTING IT IN THE HANDS OF YOU AND THOSE *JAMES BOND REJECTS* YOU RAMROD!

I WANTED THE HULK'S CAPTURE TO BE STRICTLY AN *AIR FORCE SHOW!*

PRETTY *TESTY* OLD BIRD...GUESS I'D FEEL THE SAME IF SOMEONE ELSE WAS RUNG IN ON *MY* OPERATION!

BUT NONE OF THIS *SOUL-SEARCHIN'* IS GONNA BAG US THE *HULK!*

AWRIGHT, LET'S *HUSTLE!* GAS-LAUNCHING CREWS INTO THE GLIDE-SAUCER... *MOVE IT!*

WHAT'S THE *LATEST* ON FLIGHT CONDITIONS OVER TARGET AREA?

WE'RE GETTING VERY *VAGUE* READINGS, NICK... LOT OF *TURBULENCE* FOULING THINGS UP!

BUT EVEN IF IT WAS A *HURRICANE*, HE *KNOWS* HE'D STILL DO THE JOB!

WHILE, BACK IN THE AREA UNDER *QUESTION...*

TALBOT! HOW *IS* SHE?

WEAK,...BUT COMING AROUND! BEST THING WE CAN DO IS GET HER *OUT* OF HERE!

BRUCE... *BRUCE*, DARLING,...MUST SAVE BRUCE...

IF ONLY SHE WAS SAYING *MY* NAME...IF JUST *ONCE* SHE'D FEEL THAT WAY ABOUT *ME...!*

YOU SHOULD *ALL* GET AWAY AND NOT LET *ME* SLOW YOU DOWN WITH THIS *WOUNDED LEG!*

THAT *CREATURE* WILL BE OUT FROM UNDER THE CAR IN *NO TIME* AND--

THEN, BANNER'S WORDS *DIE* IN THE SUDDEN DRYNESS OF HIS THROAT AS RADIATING *HEAT* SEARS HIS BACK, MAKING HIM TURN WITH *HORROR* TO FACE...

THE *BEAST-MAN!* WE'RE TOO *LATE*, BRUCE!

YOU CAN STILL *MAKE IT*, RICK! RUN! *RUN!!*

4

THEN, TWO BANDS OF *WHITE-HOT STEEL* REACH OUT TO ENCIRCLE BANNER'S WRISTS...

NOW... PINK-SKIN *OR* GREEN-SKIN...

YOU *PAY* FOR DARING TO *ATTACK* ME!

RICK, *PLEASE!* BEFORE THE RADIATION HITS YOU...*GO!*

NO, BRUCE... I *CAN'T*...

LISTEN TO HIM, SON! THE HELICOPTER WE CAME IN ISN'T *FAR*...

I *MUST* HAVE YOUR HELP TO GET BETTY IN AND *AIRBORNE!*

BUT AS THE INFLAMED GRIP *SCORCHES* THE YOUNG SCIENTIST WITH A *RADIOACTIVE FLOOD*, THE NEUTRALIZING EFFECT OF MR. FANTASTIC'S DEVICE IS GRADUALLY *COUNTERED*, UNTIL, ONCE *AGAIN*...

WHEN I FOUGHT THE BEAST-MAN AS THE *HULK*, HIS RADIATION TRANSFERRED ME BACK INTO *BANNER*...

BUT NOW... SINCE I WAS IN *HUMAN* FORM...HIS PRESENCE IS INSTEAD CHANGING ME INTO—

THE HULK!

WOK!

MONSTER WITH *BURNING TOUCH* NOT HOLD *HULK*...

NOTHING HOLDS THE *HULK!*

AWWRRR!

HE WON'T *NEED* ME NOW...

WHEN HE'S LIKE THIS, THERE ISN'T ANYTHING *ANYONE* CAN DO FOR HIM...OR *WITH* HIM!

5

[107]

TOO MUCH SEARING *CONTACT* WITH GLOWING CREATURE EARLIER MADE HULK BECOME *BRUCE BANNER...*

DON'T WANT THAT TO HAPPEN AGAIN... *EVER!*

IF RADIATION FLAMING *INSIDE* BEAST-MAN MAKE IT TOO DANGEROUS FOR HULK TO *HANG ON...*

...THEN HULK *LET GO!*

NOW BURNING GIANT LEARNS WHAT HAPPENS TO *ALL* WHO DEFY *HULK!*

BUT, THE RAMPANT RADIO-ACTIVE POWER WITHIN THE PRIMORDIAL BODY IS NOT SO *EASILY* EXTINGUISHED...

SUDDEN *CHANGE* OF WEAK PINK ONE INTO MIGHTY GREEN ONE WAS *SURPRISE--*

LET HIM HURL ME THRU *WALL--* INTO *BUILDING--!*

CAN NEVER KNOW *PEACE* WHILE SUCH AN ENEMY *LIVES...*

ONCE AND FOR ALL, GREEN-SKIN MUST BE *DESTROYED!*

WILL DO TO *HIM* WHAT HE TRIED WITH *ME...*I WILL *BURY* HIM!

7

BUT THE *GREEN GOLIATH* SHRUGS AWAY THE SHATTERED RUBBLE AROUND HIM, AND ANGRILY *LEAPS...*

BEAST-MAN MAKE *MISTAKE!* SHOULD HAVE STAYED *STILL...*

MAYBE THEN HULK THINK HE'S SMASHED FOR *GOOD...*

NOW, THE *BURNING ONE* FIND OUT WHAT BATTLE WITH HULK *REALLY* IS!

UNNGHHHH!

HULK KEEP FORGETTING WOUND IN *LEG...CAN'T* JUMP *ALL* THE WAY!

KRUNCH

BUT EVEN IF HULK *CAN'T LEAP...*

...HE CAN STILL *CLIMB!*

MONSTER NOT GO *AWAY...HULK* IS *COMING!*

AND SO-- POUNDING, CLAWING HOLDS FROM CRACKING *CONCRETE* AND CRUMBLING *MORTAR--* THE HULK STALKS FLY-LIKE TOWARD HIS *BESTIAL FOE...*

HOWEVER, THE *RADIO-ACTIVE SURVIVOR* OF EONS PAST DOES DOES NOT IDLY AWAIT ATTACK...

NOW! WILL DRIVE GREAT GREEN ENEMY DOWN TO BE *CRUSHED* ON GROUND BELOW!

AARGHN!

CREATURE HITS WITH *SLAMMING FORCE--*AND *BURNING, SCORCHING TOUCH!*

WOM!

BUT, HULK CAN STILL *POUND HIM* AS WE FALL!

YET, NEITHER OF THE *TUMBLING TITANS* IS TO LEARN HIS FATE IN THE LONG FALL...

...FOR, AT THAT VERY *INSTANT,* THEY ARE *ENGULFED* BY A SUCTIONING SWIRL OF BLAZING ENERGY, LIFTING THEM UP...*UP...*

8

AND, TRIUMPHANTLY, ON THE SCENE IN THE STREET BELOW... *GENERAL THUNDERBOLT ROSS*...

BY HEAVEN, THEY *DID* IT!

MUCH AS I *HATE* HAVING ANYONE BUT *ME* BRING THAT BLASTED *BRUTE* TO BAY--

SO LONG AS THOSE MONSTERS ARE *GONE*, SIR, I GUESS IT DOESN'T MATTER *WHO* DID IT!

I'VE GOT TO GIVE *FURY* AND THOSE CLOAK 'N' *DAGGER* CLOWNS FROM SHIELD *CREDIT!*

BEFORE THE PLEASED ON-LOOKERS, BOTH OF THE *FORMIDABLE FORMS* ARE LIFTED SKYWARD...

BUT, NOW THAT I *THINK* OF IT, SIR...WASN'T FURY SUPPOSED TO BE *USING* SOME KIND OF *SAUCERS...* AND AN EXPERI- MENTAL *GAS?*

THIS LOOKS LIKE SHIELD'S *HEADQUARTERS SHIP* AND THAT *VORTEX BEAM* OF THEIRS!

OFFICER, I DON'T CARE IF THEY SPRAY HIM WITH *INCENSE* AND LEAD HIM AWAY SINGING *HARE KRISHNA*...

JUST SO THE *HULK* IS FINALLY OUT OF MY HAIR FOR *GOOD!*

OS, SMITH & CO.

IT WOULD SEEM GENERAL ROSS HAS BEEN GRANTED HIS *WISH*, AS THE WHIRLING, LUMINOUS *FORCE* DRAWS THE HULK AND HIS CRYSTALLINE OPPONENT INTO THE *MECHANICAL COMPLEXITY* OF THE BEAMING CHAMBER...

STRANGE LIGHT *PULLS* HULK INTO AIR--AGAINST HIS *WILL!*

NOTHING CAN DO THAT TO HULK!

BUT, BEAM KEEPS HULK OFF *BALANCE*... CAN'T *SMASH MACHINERY!*

AND, WHILE THE TWIN TITANS ARE HELD IN HELPLESS RAGE BY THE SWIRLING ENERGY, THE HUGE SHIP MOVES SUDDENLY WITH BLURRING *SPEED*...AND IS GONE IN SUCH A TWINKLING THAT ONE MIGHT THINK IT WAS NEVER THERE...

AS THE MAMMOTH CRAFT HURTLES INTO THE NIGHT, ITS GLEAMING INTERIOR SWARMS WITH *ACTIVITY*...ACTIVITY CENTERED AROUND THE TWO GROTESQUE AND INCREDIBLE *CREATURES* DRAWN FROM THE EARTH BELOW...

IN THE FLESH, THEY APPEAR FAR MORE *AWESOME*, MORE *POWERFUL* THAN I IMAGINED!

YET, THERE WAS NO *CHOICE*... IT *HAD* TO BE DONE!

FLIGHT CONTROL DECK...THIS IS *COLONEL BREVLOV!*

IMPRESSIVE *RESISTANCE!* BUT OBSERVE ...WITH SUFFICIENT CONCENTRATION, EVEN *HE* BEGINS TO FALL!

WE'VE SUBJECTED THEM TO *MAXIMUM DENSITY STUNMIST*, COLONEL-- BUT THE HULK STILL *STANDS!*

CONTINUE ALL *DETECTION-EVASION MEASURES...* BUT SET A COURSE FOR *HOME!*

AND, BACK NEAR THE SPOT WHERE THE HULK *DISAPPEARED...*

AWRIGHT, GENERAL ROSS, WE'RE *READY AN' RARIN!...*

WHERE'S THIS JOLLY-GREEN *EMERGENCY* OF YOURS?

WHERE'S THE--*WHA*--?

BLAST IT, FURY...NO NEED RUBBING IN YOUR *SUCCESS* BY PULLING MY LEG!

MEANIN' NO *DISRESPECT*, GENERAL...

BUT WHAT IN *BLAZES* ARE YA *TALKIN'* ABOUT?!

TALKING *ABOUT?!* SHIELD'S CAPTURE OF THE *HULK!* WHAT EL--?

FURY, DO YOU *MEAN* IT? THAT WASN'T *YOUR* SHIP THAT GRABBED HIM?!

WOULD I LOOK LIKE *THIS* IF IT *WAS?*

THERE'S JUST *ONE GUY* WHO COULD PULL A CAPER LIKE THIS...

DUM-DUM? *FURY!* GIMME A PRIORITY ALERT... YURI BREVLOV'S BACK IN ACTION!

AND, EVEN AS THE REDOUBTABLE LEADER OF SHIELD SPEAKS A LONG-UNSAID NAME, LET US RETURN TO THE HURTLING SUB-SPACE *CARRIER*...

KEEP THE *MAGNETIC TRANSPORTERS* MOVING... UNLESS YOU WANT TO BE AROUND WHEN THE *STUN MIST WEARS OFF!*

WE ARE MOVING AS FAST AS WE CAN, COMRADE!

COLONEL...DO YOU THINK IT IS *WISE* TO THUS EXPOSE YOURSELF TO THE BEAST-MAN'S *RADIATION?*

A *BRIEF* EXPOSURE WILL HARDLY *KILL* ME, ALEXI!

BUT, COLONEL, THE *DANGER...*

--IS HARDLY AS GREAT AS YOUR COWERING *FEAR*, BABBLER! OTHERWISE, I WOULD NOT BE SO *FOOLHARDY* AS TO APPROACH THEM!

YET, YOU TREMBLE ALMOST AS FEARFULLY AS OUR *ACCURSED* ORIENTAL *COMRADES!*

I....I DO NOT *UNDERSTAND*, COLONEL....!

"HAVE YOU FORGOTTEN THAT WE LEARNED HOW THEY TRANSPORTED THE BEAST-MAN TO *NEW YORK*...AFRAID THEY COULD NOT CONTROL HIS RAMPAGING *POWER?*"

"YET, NOW, THEY HAVE SEEN THEIR *ERROR*...AND ARE TRYING TO *DUPLICATE* HIM, BY EXPERIMENTATION ON *APES...!*"

THUS FAR, THEY HAVE BEEN WHOLLY *UNSUCCESSFUL*...BUT WHAT IF THEY ACHIEVE A SUDDEN *BREAKTHROUGH?*

WITH AN *ARMY* OF SUCH CREATURES, THEY MIGHT *EVEN* TURN ON US!

BUT, WHAT OF THE *HULK?* WHY DO WE NOT DESTROY *HIM*, AT LEAST?

YOUR SHORTSIGHTEDNESS NEVER CEASES TO *AMAZE* ME, ALEXI!

THE *HULK*, TOO, IS THE RESULT OF AN ACCIDENT CONCERNING *RADIO-ACTIVITY!*

HE MAY EVEN HOLD THE KEY TO THE *BEAST-MAN'S* CREATION!

11

"EVEN NOW, THE AMERICANS MUST *KNOW* THAT THE TWO BEHEMOTHS ARE IN OUR HANDS..."

NO DOUBT ABOUT IT, NICK...THE FOREIGN CARRIER'S *FLOWN THE COOP!*

IT ELUDED OUR *RADAR*...AND WAS SPOTTED OVER THE *ARCTIC!*

BLAST THE CRUMMY LUCK!

WE'VE WANTED FOR *MONTHS* TO GET THIS CLOSE TO CATCHING THAT CREEP, AND *NOW...*

BUT SUDDENLY, ABOARD THE SPEEDING CRAFT, BREVLOV'S MUSINGS ARE *INTERRUPTED*, AS...

COLONEL...OUR SHIP...IT'S WILDLY *CAREENING!*

WHAT COULD BE *CAUSING* IT?

CAN'T YOU *GUESS*, ALEXI?

ONLY *ONE* FACTOR COULD HAVE CAUSED SUCH A THING...

OUR TWO UNHUMAN PRISONERS ...HAVE *AWAKENED!*

AND, YURI BREVLOV KNOWS WHEREOF HE *SPEAKS*...FOR AT THAT MOMENT, WITHIN A HIGHLY-REINFORCED *CUBICLE...*

THEY HAVE TRIED TO *IMPRISON* ME!

MUST BREAK *FREE*... THEN... *KILL*... *KILL*...!

WHILE, IN AN ADJOINING, EVEN MORE *HEAVILY*, STEEL-LINED CHAMBER...

HAH! THEY PUT HULK IN *CHAINS!*

BUT, *NO* CHAINS EVER MADE CAN HOLD *HULK!*

SNAP!

AND, *NO ONE* KEEPS HULK... WHERE HE DOESN'T WANT TO *STAY!*

RRIPP!

NO! IT... IT CAN'T BE--!

SOUND THE ALARM! BRING MORE STUN-MIST GUNS... *ANYTHING!*

THE HULK HAS BROKEN FREE!!

COULD *STOP* THAT PUNY ONE...IF NOT FOR WOUNDED *LEG*...!

12

STILL, WITH EVERY SECOND, MORE *POWER* RETURNS TO IT!

SOON, HULK WILL BE *ALL RIGHT* AGAIN, AND THEN--

BUT, WHAT *PLACE* IS THIS? WHERE *AM I?*

YET, WHILE THE HULK THUS *PONDERS,* THE VESSEL'S *COMMANDER* IS ALREADY TAKING ACTION...

THE HULK MUST BE *RECAPTURED...IF* POSSIBLE, *ALIVE...* BUT IF *NOT...!*

THE SHIP'S *INTER-COM* IS NOW OPEN, COLONEL!

EXCELLENT! HAND ME THE *COMMUNI-CATOR!*

ATTENTION! ALL HANDS OUT OF THE *FORWARD SECTION...* AT ONCE!

IT WILL BE *SEALED OFF...* IN *TWENTY SECONDS!*

BAH! HULK DOES NOT *CARE* ENOUGH TO HURT *THEM!*

WANT TO FIND *GLOWING MONSTER...* FINISH OUR *BATTLE...!*

HOWEVER, JUST NOW, THE SAVAGE, UNTAMED BRUTE FOR WHOM THE HULK SEARCHES IS HIMSELF A HELPLESS *PRISONER...*

...A RAGING CAPTIVE WHO HAS GROWN TOO *WEAK* TO DO ANYTHING...BUT *REMEMBER...*

IT REMEMBERS A TIME COUNTLESS MILLENNIA *PAST,* WHEN IT HAD BEEN ONE OF THE NEAR-HUMAN, NEANDERTHALOID BEINGS STRUGGLING FOR *LIFE* UPON A MERCILESS EARTH...

IT REMEMBERS THE SEETHING *VOLCANIC BLAST* WHICH *BURIED* IT...

...AND THE FIERY *MUSHROOM CLOUD* THAT RELEASED IT FROM ITS *SUSPENDED STATE...*

BUT, IN BETWEEN, IT REMEMBERS THE DISMAL, ENDLESS *DARKNESS* WHICH HAD ENCOMPASSED IT...

...AND WHICH NOW ENSHROUDS IT ONCE MORE WITHIN A GRIM, GREY WALL OF UNBEARABLE *SILENCE...*

13

MEANWHILE, *UNAWARE* OF HIS RECENT FOE'S LOCATION, THE GREEN-SKINNED *HULK* CAN ONLY RAGE AGAINST THE CONFINING *CARRIER...*

WE SEALED OFF THE FORWARD SECTION... *TOO LATE!*

THE HULK'S *BREAKING THRU* THE WALL...LIKE SOME HUMAN *SLEDGE-HAMMER!*

SMASH

WHERE IS THE ONE HULK *SEEKS?*

TELL ME...OR I'LL *DESTROY* THE SHIP... PIECE BY PIECE!

BACK... STAY *BACK!!*

IF ONLY THIS *STUN-MIST* PISTOL WILL STOP HIM...!

ONCE *BEFORE,* STRANGE FOG SURROUNDED ME...*CAPTURED* ME!

THIS TIME, I WON'T *LET* IT SURROUND ME...I'LL JUMP OUT OF ITS *WAY!*

SUDDENLY, HAVING RIPPED HIS WAY THRU THE SOLID-STEEL CEILING, THE GREEN GOLIATH *RECALLS...*

HULK'S *JUMPING POWERS* HAVE RETURNED ALMOST AS *STRONG* AS EVER!

THEN, MUST TEAR THRU *OUTER HULL* OF THIS PLACE...

...SO HULK CAN LEAP TO *SAFETY...* FIND HIS *ENEMY...*

I...I DON'T *BELIEVE* IT!

HE WRENCHED LOOSE THAT *FUEL TANK...* AND *HURLED* IT LIKE A BULLET!

THIS IS *EASIEST* WAY TO SMASH THRU HULL!

STRANGELY ENOUGH, THE HULK DOES NOT REALIZE THAT HIS HEAVY PRO-JECTILE IS VIRTUALLY A TRIGGERED *BOMB,* UNTIL...

PHROOM!

LOOK OUT! IT *EXPLODED...* THE SHIP'S ON FIRE!

14

GET THE *CHEMICAL EXTINGUISHERS*... QUICKLY!

BUT, WHAT ABOUT THE *HULK*?

WHAM!

FORGET HIM FOR NOW... BEFORE WE CRASH!

BUT, THERE IS *ONE* MAN ABOARD THE BESIEGED CRAFT WHO CANNOT...*WILL NOT* FORGET THE GREEN-SKINNED TITAN...

THIS IS *COLONEL BREVLOV!*

CREWS *ONE* AND *TWO* SECURE FORWARD SECTOR... WHILE OTHERS CLOSE IN ON THE *HULK!*

BUT, WHERE *IS* HE NOW, COMRADE COLONEL?

WAIT! THERE-- ON THE *SCREEN!*

THE *HULK* IS *OUT-SIDE* THE SHIP!

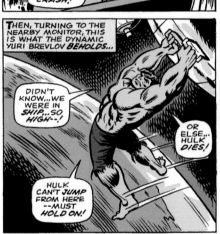

THEN, TURNING TO THE NEARBY MONITOR, THIS IS WHAT THE DYNAMIC YURI BREVLOV *BEHOLDS*...

DIDN'T KNOW... WE WERE IN *SHIP*... SO *HIGH*--!

OR ELSE... HULK *DIES!*

HULK CAN'T *JUMP* FROM HERE --MUST *HOLD ON!*

AND, JUST TO *COMPLETE* OUR LITTLE ROLL CALL--LOOK WHAT'S HAPPENED TO OUR SOMEWHAT BELABORED *BEAST-MAN*...

I AM...*FREE*-- FREED BY SOME MIGHTY *BLAST!*

MUST FIND THOSE WHO *CAGED* ME... *DESTROY* THEM!

MEANWHILE, HOWEVER, THE VESSEL'S CREW HAVE *OTHER* THINGS TO WORRY ABOUT...

THESE *MAGNETIC SOLES* WILL ENABLE ME TO *REACH* THE HULK ...OUT THERE!

BUT--WHY *YOU*, COLONEL? WHY NOT *ANOTHER*?

THE HULK IS *MY* RESPONSIBILITY, ALEXI--

I SHALL BRING HIM *BACK* WITH ME--

--OR *I* MYSELF SHALL *NOT* RETURN!

THEN, AS THE COLONEL EXITS THRU AN *OPEN HATCH*...

OUR LEADER IS *BRAVE* BEYOND WORDS!

BRAVE, PERHAPS ...BUT ALSO *FOOL-HARDY!*

NO MATTER *WHAT* HIS ORDERS...WE MUST *HELP* HIM--!

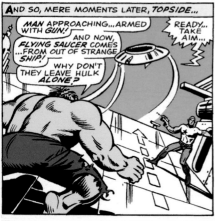

AND SO, MERE MOMENTS LATER, *TOPSIDE...*

MAN APPROACHING...ARMED WITH *GUN!*

AND NOW, *FLYING SAUCER* COMES ...FROM OUT OF STRANGE *SHIP!*

WHY DON'T THEY LEAVE HULK *ALONE?*

READY... TAKE AIM...

FIRE!

WHAT--? THOSE INFERNAL *FOOLS...!*

PTHAK!

I TOLD THEM *I* WOULD HANDLE THIS! BUT *NOW--*

WAIT! THE IMPACT OF THAT SHELL... *DISLODGED* ME FROM THE HULL!

I'M *FALLING...* FALLING TO MY *DEATH--!*

HAH! HULK CAUGHT HOLD OF *BOTTOM* OF SHIP!

BUT, CAN'T *REACH* MAN WITH GUN!

BY COMING TO ATTACK HULK, HE SEALED HIS OWN *DOOM!*

BUT, JUST THEN, INSIDE THE SHIP, A FRIGHTENING, TOTALLY *UNEXPECTED* PHENOMENON IS OCCURRING...

FEEL... *STRANGE...* LIKE NEVER, *BEFORE....*

FOR, DURING HIS PAST BATTLES, AN EVER-INCREASING *CHAIN-REACTION* HAS BEEN BUILDING UP INSIDE THE WALKING ATOMIC PILE KNOWN AS THE *BEAST-MAN...*

CAN'T *STAND* IT... ANY MORE...

PAIN... INSIDE HEAD... GROWING *WORSE...*

...UNTIL SUDDENLY, A STARTLING *REALIZATION* BURSTS UPON THE CREATURE'S THROBBING BRAIN...

GOING TO *DIE!*

GOING TO DIE-- *NOW!!*

JUST THEN, AS THE ANXIOUS CREWMAN IS IN *MID-SENTENCE*...

HE *JUMPED*--!

SAUCER HAD DIPPED *DOWN*... CLOSER TO THE *GROUND*!

HULK CAN *SURVIVE* THE FALL NOW....!

MADE IT! BUT NOW... SAUCER IS *FIRING* AT HULK!

FRUMI

IT *MISSED*... HIT *FARM-HOUSE* NEARBY....!

WHAT THE HULK CAN'T *KNOW*... IS THAT I *TRIED* TO MISS HIM!

WITH THE *BEAST-MAN* DESTROYED, WE CAN GAIN LITTLE MORE BY HARMING THAT TORTURED GREEN *GARGOYLE*!

GIVE THE *COMMAND*, COMRADE! PREPARE TO *ABANDON CHASE*!

ABAN--?

BUT, OUR ORDERS WERE TO SEE THOSE TWO MONSTERS *CAPTURED*... OR *OBLITERATED*!

TO *SPARE* ONE OF THEM NOW WOULD BE... AN ACT OF *TREASON*!

HE'S *RIGHT!* I WOULD SOON HAVE A *MUTINY* ON MY HANDS!

I MUST DECIDE WHAT TO DO ...*QUICKLY*!

FOR A FATEFUL, TORMENTED SECOND, THE FOREIGN COUNTERPART OF *NICK FURY* WEIGHS HIS DREAD CHOICES IN HIS STEEL-TRAP MIND! THEN...

THERE IS ONLY ONE *CHOICE*!

THE *HULK* MUST *DIE*!

WHILE, BELOW, SOME UNCANNY *SIXTH SENSE* SEEMS TO HAVE DRIVEN THE GARGANTUAN HULK TO APPROACH NEARER...EVER *NEARER*... THE FLAMING FARMHOUSE...

HULK *HEARD* SOMETHING... SOMEONE *CRY OUT*....!

THERE IS THE ONE I HEARD--!

18

IT'S...A *MAN-CHILD!* ONE OF THE RACE THAT *HOUNDS* THE HULK...!

HE *LOOKS UP* AT HULK...*SEES* HULK!

BUT...HE ISN'T *AFRAID.!!*

MAN-CHILD'S PARENTS MUST HAVE *FLED* WHEN SAUCER FIRED, AND--

WAIT! HULK JUST *REMEMBERED* THE SAUCER!

IT'S SWOOPING LOW EVEN NOW ...TO *ATTACK.*

THIS IS *HULK'S* FIGHT...NOT *MAN-CHILD'S!*

MUST *LEAVE* HIM... OR HE'LL BE KILLED WHEN IT *FIRES!*

YET, HE'S SO *HELPLESS* ...SO *ALONE!**

*EVEN IF THE YOUNGSTER *SPOKE* ALOUD, OUR GREEN-SKINNED GOLEM COULDN'T UNDERSTAND HIS *LANGUAGE*...BUT THE *EYES* OF CHILDREN SPEAK A TONGUE *BEYOND* LANGUAGE!--STAN.

YES...HE'S *ALONE...* ALONE, JUST LIKE THE *HULK!*

STILL, WHY SHOULD *I WORRY* ABOUT HIM...*PUNIEST* OF THE RACE THAT *TORMENTS* ME!

PITY IS FOR *HUMANS...* NOT FOR *HULK!*

BUT, THE NEXT SECOND...

...THE PLUMMETING *SAUCER- SHIP* FIRES A LETHAL BLAST ...AND THE CREATURE WHO WAS ONCE *BRUCE BANNER* LEAPS OUT OF HARM'S WAY...

ZKOK!

...INSTINCTIVELY CARRYING THE *BOY* TO SAFETY WITH HIM!

WE *MISSED*...BUT, I HAVE A PLAN WHICH CAN HARDLY *FAIL!*

YET, WHAT WAS THE SMALL *BUNDLE* HE CARRIED...SO TENDERLY IN HIS MASSIVE ARMS?

WHAT DOES IT *MATTER,* MY COLONEL?

ALL THAT MATTERS IS THAT WE *DESTROY THE HULK* ...AS WE WERE *COMMANDED!*

19

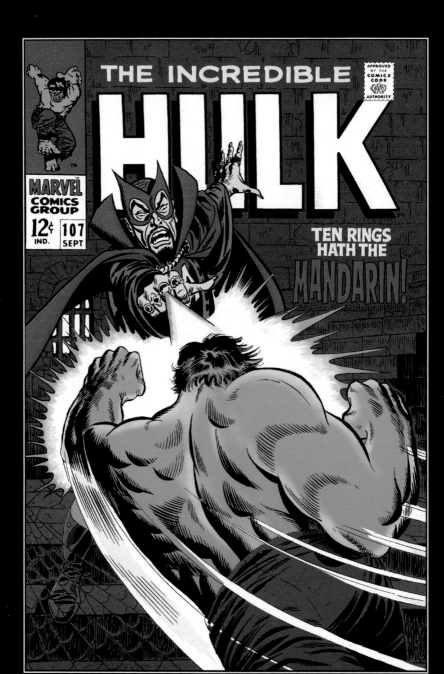

THE INCREDIBLE HULK! ™

TEN RINGS HATH...

CAUGHT DEAD IN THE SIGHTS OF RUSSIAN SECRET SERVICE COLONEL YURI BREVLOV, THE HULK RISKS HIS VERY EXISTENCE TO SAVE THE LIFE OF A HELPLESS CHILD—HIS CLOUDED BRAIN UNABLE TO COMPREHEND THE SIMPLE FACT THAT HIS ACTIONS CAN ONLY LEAD THEM BOTH TO...CERTAIN DOOM!!

THE MANDARIN!

BUT, JUST IN CASE YOU THINK...

| STAN LEE, EDITOR | GARY FRIEDRICH, WRITER | HERB TRIMPE, ARTIST | SYD SHORES, INKER | AND | ARTIE SIMEK, LETTERER... |

HAVE BITTEN OFF MORE THAN OL' GREEN-SKIN CAN CHEW THIS TIME, JUST TURN THE PAGE AND FIND OUT HOW WRONG YOU CAN BE...

IT IS *NO USE*, COLONEL!

OUR SHOTS MERELY BOUNCE *OFF* HIM...AND MAKE HIM MORE *ANGRY!*

SURELY, SIR, YOU REALIZE THAT OUR ONLY COURSE OF ACTION IS... THE *UNI-DISINTEGRATOR!*

DO YOU THINK I AM NOT *AWARE* OF THAT? YET, I CAN'T BRING MYSELF TO HARM THE *CHILD!*

BUT...GOOD LORD! HE'S ATTACKING US!

I MUST MAKE ONE LAST ATTEMPT TO STOP HIM WITH OUR *CONVENTIONAL ARMAMENT!*

HULK WILL *SMASH* THOSE WHO SHOOT AT HIM!

HOWEVER, JUST AS THE ENRAGED *BEHEMOTH* SOARS TO WITHIN *REACH* OF THE SOVIET CRAFT...

ZAK!

:UUUNNNHHHH!:

PUNY WEAPONS ONLY *STING* HULK!

THEY CAN'T *STOP* ME!

BUT, AS THE RUSSIAN COUNTERPART TO *NICK FURY* PRESSES THE TRIGGER ONCE MORE...

KA·ZAT!

:AARRGGGHHH!:

AND, WITHIN SECONDS, THE GREAT GREEN *GARGOYLE* IS DRIVEN BACK TO *EARTH*...

THEIR WEAPONS ARE STRONGER THAN HULK *THOUGHT*...

...BUT NOT NEARLY STRONG ENOUGH TO *KILL* ME!

WHILE, A THOUSAND FEET *OVERHEAD*...

I CANNOT DELAY MY ACTION ANY *LONGER!*

HE LOOKS AS THOUGH HE'S GETTING READY TO *ATTACK* AGAIN! SO IT'S EITHER HIM AND THE *BOY*...OR MY SHIP AND *CREW!*

CLEARLY, I MUST USE THE *UNI-DISINTEGRATOR* AGAINST HIM!

PREPARE WEAPON-U FOR IMMEDIATE FIRING!

2

WHILE, BELOW...

GO AHEAD AND *FIRE* MORE BULLETS AT HULK! I'M NOT *AFRAID* OF YOU!

YOU TRY TO *HARM* HULK...AND MY *FRIEND!* BUT IT WON'T DO YOU ANY *GOOD!*

NO WEAPON ON *EARTH* CAN KILL ME...DO YOU *HEAR?* THE HULK CAN'T BE *STOPPED!*

ALL CIRCUITS ARE *FUNCTIONING,* COLONEL! WEAPON-U READY FOR *FIRING!*

THEN, I CANNOT *STALL* ANY LONGER! BEGIN FIRING *COUNTDOWN!*

I WILL MAN THE...*WAIT...* I SMELL *SMOKE!*

AND, A FRACTION OF A SECOND LATER, THE CRAFT IS ROCKED BY A JOLTING *EXPLOSION...*

WE'RE UNDER *ATTACK!*

ALL HANDS TO THE *ESCAPE HATCH!*

THEN, AS THE CRIPPLED SHIP SPINS DIZZILY TOWARD THE *GROUND,* ITS ATTACKER SWOOPS DOWN TO FOLLOW THE *DEADLY DESCENT...*

...ITS CREW GRIMLY FOLLOWING THE TERRIBLE TABLEAU ON A *VIEWSCREEN...*

MAN THE *VORTEX BEAM!* I WANT THAT RUSKY SAUCER SET DOWN ON THE GROUND GENTLE AS A *CRADLE!*

I DON'T WANT A MAN ABOARD *HURT!*

YOU LOST YER *MIND,* NICK? FIRST YA SHOOT 'EM *DOWN* --THEN YA TELL US TO *SAVE* 'EM!

I'M *RUNNIN'* THIS SHOW, YA OL' *WALRUS!* SO JUST KEEP YER EYES PEELED... AND YER YAPPER *SHUT!*

3

BUT, EVEN AS THE SCIENTIFIC GENIUS OF *SHIELD* IS *SPARING* THE SOVIET SHIP...

THAT STRANGE LIGHT...IT'S KEEPING HULK'S ENEMIES FROM *CRASHING!*

BUT THE LIGHT WON'T HELP THEM FOR *LONG!* ONLY UNTIL HULK CAN *REACH* THEM!

THEY *CAPTURED* HULK... AND BROUGHT ME TO THIS STRANGE LAND!* THEN TRIED TO *KILL* ME!

NOW HULK WILL MAKE THEM *SORRY* FOR IT!

*AS PEERLESSLY PORTRAYED IN OUR *LAST* ILLUSTRIOUS ISH! --SET-IT-STRAIGHT STAN.

AND, INDEED, BEFORE THE STARTLED RUSSIANS CAN *FLEE* THEIR CRIPPLED CRAFT...

THE HULK STRIKES...

IT...IT'S *HIM!* HE'S ATTACKING... RIPPING THE SHIP *APART!*

WE'RE BEING HURTLED THROUGH THE AIR...LIKE MERE *DOLLS!*

YOU TRIED TO DESTROY HULK... SO NOW HULK WILL DESTROY *YOU!*

PUNY HUMANS *HATE* HULK WHEN THEY HAVE *GUNS* TO SHOOT AT ME...

...BUT, *WITHOUT* THEIR GUNS, THEY CAN ONLY FEEL *FEAR!*

4

BUT, AFTER THE *REMAINDER* OF THE SOVIET CREW HAS FLED IN *STARK PANIC...*

ENEMY LEADER IS *HURT...* BEGS HULK FOR MERCY!

YOU...YOU MUST *LISTEN* TO ME! I *DID NOT WISH* TO *HARM...*

BUT HE'LL GET NO *MORE PITY* THAN HE SHOWED HULK!

BUT, AS THE HULK LUNGES TOWARD HIS *QUARRY...*

WHA....?!

HULK WILL....! HE'S *GONE...* SLIPPED FROM HULK'S GRASP!

STRANGE LIGHT PULLS HIM TOWARD *FLYING MACHINE* ABOVE ME!

GREETIN'S, BREVLOV! HOW'S *TRICKS?*

HUH? YA MEAN YOU *KNOW* 'IM?

GOOD MORNING, COLONEL FURY! NICE OF YOU TO *DROP BY!**

*JUST IN CASE YOU'RE WONDERING WHAT THE *CONNECTION* IS BETWEEN FURY AND BREVLOV, ALL WE CAN TELL YOU NOW IS...TUNE IN *NEXT ISH!* WE'RE GONNA BE TIED UP WITH OUR JOLLY GREEN GOLEM FOR THE REST OF *THIS ONE!*   -- SALESMAN STAN.

LET'S JUST SAY IT WUZ A GOOD THING I WUZ IN THE *NEIGHBORHOOD,* YURI!

I CANNOT DENY THAT--AND I SUPPOSE IT WOULD BE *UN-GRATEFUL* FOR ME TO ASK *WHY* YOU HAPPEN TO BE FLYING OVER SOVIET TERRITORY?!

YOU *BET'CH'RE* SOLJER SUIT IT WOULD! DUM DUM, TAKE THE PRISONER TO HIS *QUARTERS!*

SO...SOMEONE'S CHEATED HULK OUT OF HIS *REVENGE!* BUT, IT WON'T BE FOR *LONG...*

...HULK WILL GO *AFTER* THEM...AND NOTHING CAN STOP ME!

NOTHING, THAT IS, SAVE THE MAD SCIENTIFIC GENIUS OF A MAN THOUSANDS OF MILES AWAY...IN A REMOTE SECTION OF *COMMUNIST CHINA...*

...A MAN WHO CAREFULLY WATCHES THE HULK'S EVERY MOVE, HIS MIND *WHIRLING* WITH YET ANOTHER OF HIS SINISTER SCHEMES FOR WORLD DOMINATION...

...A MAN KNOWN TO THE WORLD AS...

5

THE MANDARIN... HAS AT LAST FOUND THE MEANS BY WHICH TO ACHIEVE HIS *ETERNAL GOAL!*

WITH THE UNWITTING AID OF THE GREEN-SKINNED GARGOYLE CALLED *THE HULK--* THE WORLD WILL SOON BE *MINE!*

YOU...FOLLOW ME TO THE TELEPORTATIONAL CENTER! THERE IS *WORK* TO BE DONE!

WITHIN BUT A FEW SHORT HOURS, THE RE-COLONIZATION OF EARTH WILL BE *UNDERWAY!*

A SINGLE BURST FROM MY *ULTRA-HIGH FREQUENCY RING* WILL PERMANENTLY LOCK MY VIEW-SCREEN TO HIS EVERY *MOVEMENT!*

...SO THAT, WHEN THE MOMENT TO *SUMMON* HIM ARRIVES, THERE WILL BE NO PROBLEM IN *LOCATING* HIM!

THEN, AS A FULL MOON CASTS ITS SHIMMERING SILVER BEAMS ACROSS THE VAST EXPANSE OF THE *GOBI DESERT...*

...A MODERN COMPLEX, STANDING OUT LIKE A LONE *OASIS*, BECOMES A BEEHIVE OF ACTIVITY... SURROUNDED BY AN EERIE AURA OF...*EVIL.*

AND, AT THAT SAME MOMENT, THOUSANDS OF MILES *AWAY...*

MY FRIEND IS *TIRED... HUNGRY,...*

MAYBE HULK CAN FIND FOOD IN THAT *VILLAGE!*

EVEN IF PEOPLE *HATE* HULK... I MUST THINK OF MY FRIEND *FIRST!*

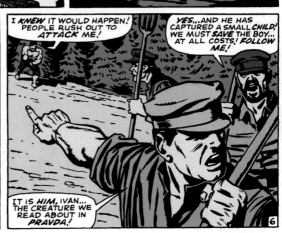

I *KNEW* IT WOULD HAPPEN! PEOPLE RUSH OUT TO *ATTACK* ME!

*YES...*AND HE HAS CAPTURED A SMALL *CHILD!* WE MUST *SAVE* THE BOY... AT ALL COSTS! *FOLLOW ME!*

IT IS *HIM,* IVAN... THE CREATURE WE READ ABOUT IN *PRAVDA!*

6

"PUT THE CHILD *DOWN*, YOU *SAVAGE!*"

"THEY DON'T *UNDERSTAND!* THEY THINK HULK WANTS TO *HARM THE BOY!*"

"HE SEEMS *FRIGHTENED...* CONFUSED!"

"FOOLS! THE HULK FEARS *NOTHING!*"

"THEN STOP USING A CHILD AS A *SHIELD!*"

"I *WILL* PUT HIM DOWN...BUT ONLY TO KEEP HIM FROM GETTING *HURT!* HULK DOESN'T *NEED* A SHIELD!"

"LOOK! HE'S *DOING* IT! HE'S PUT THE BOY *ASIDE!*"

"NOW LET'S *FINISH* THE MONSTER! COME ON!"

"HULK'S FRIEND IS *SAFE* NOW! HULK IS READY TO *FIGHT!*"

"IF PUNY MEN WANT *BATTLE...* HULK WILL *GIVE* IT TO THEM!"

"WAIT!"

"WHAT? NO ONE ORDERS HULK TO..."

"PLEASE! YOU'RE MY FRIEND...BUT SO ARE *THEY!*"

"DON'T *HURT* THEM! PLEASE!"

"THE BOY DOESN'T SEEM TO BE *AFRAID!*"

"IS WHAT HE SAYS *TRUE*...THAT YOU'VE *BEFRIENDED* HIM?"

7.

WITHOUT A WORD, THE HULK LUMBERS THRU THE CROWD, WHICH PARTS LIKE A LIVING *FEARFUL SEA*--

NONE INTERFERE AS THE HULK, WITH HEAVY, PONDEROUS TREAD, STORMS INTO THE GATHERING *DARKNESS*...

HIS FIGURE GROWS DIMMER--DIMMER-- WHEN--

SUDDENLY--

ZA SP

HE *VANISHED!* BUT--*HOW?*

INSTANTANEOUSLY, AT THE STRONGHOLD OF--THE *MANDARIN*--

AHHH, YOU HAVE *ARRIVED!* AND...YOU'RE MORE *MAGNIFICENT* THAN I HAD DARED *HOPE!*

THE AWESOME *SIZE*...THE SHEER BRUTE *STRENGTH*... THE DEFIANT *HATRED* IN YOUR EYES!

WHERE AM I? WHO PLAYS *TRICKS* ON HULK?

PATIENCE, HELPLESS ONE! IN TIME ALL WILL BE MADE *CLEAR* TO YOU!

FIRST, THOUGH, I WISH TO *TEST*...JUST TO BE *CERTAIN* YOU ARE THE ONE I *SEEK!*

NO ONE TELLS *HULK* TO WAIT!

FIZZACHT

THAT IS WHERE YOU ARE *WRONG,* YOU DIM-WITTED GARGOYLE... AS YOU SOON WILL *SEE!*

FIRST, I SHALL TEST YOUR *REFLEXES*... AS MY *POWER* RING ACTIVATES A HIDDEN *LEVER*--

8

WHAT'S THIS? COULD I HAVE BEEN *WRONG?* HE CONTINUES TO RANT AND RAVE WHILE CERTAIN *DEATH* HURTLES EVER *CLOSER,* TO HIM!

HULK DIDN'T *ASK* TO COME HERE! SEND ME BACK... OR HULK WILL *DESTROY* YOU!

RAWK!

HAH! HULK *FOOLED* YOU! YOU THOUGHT YOU HAD *TRAPPED* HULK!

BUT NOW HULK WILL SHOW YOU WHO THE *REAL* FOOL IS!

INCREDIBLE! HIS REFLEXES ARE WITHOUT *EQUAL!* STILL, HE MUST BE TESTED *FURTHER!*

NOW I WILL TEST YOUR RESISTANCE TO THE *UNKNOWN...*

...BY ENGULFING YOU IN AN *INVISIBLE, ELECTRONIC* FORCE FIELD!

AGGGH!

MUST BREAK *FREE...* BUT *HOW?*

UNLESS I CAN SHATTER THE CONCRETE BY...

...SMASHING IT AGAINST THE *FLOOR!*

CRASH!

IT WORKED!

NOW HULK IS FREE TO *FIGHT BACK!*

WHOOM!

YOU DON'T EVEN *KNOW* HULK... YET YOU TRY TO *KILL* ME!

YOU'RE LIKE ALL *OTHER* MEN... ALWAYS *HOUNDING* HULK!

BUT HULK WON'T *TAKE* ANY MORE! NOW HULK WILL *FIGHT BACK!*

HE'S FAR STRONGER THAN EVEN *I* HAD ANTICIPATED...

...HE'S RIPPED THE VERY FLOOR ON WHICH I STAND FROM UNDER MY *FEET!*

YOU ARE HULK'S *ENEMY...* AND HULK CAN NEVER REST WHILE ENEMIES *LIVE!*

SO NOW HULK WILL CRUSH YOU LIKE A *FLY!*

BUT... WHAT'S *THAT?* THE MASKED MAN WAS JUST... A *ROBOT!*

THAT MEANS MAN WHO TRIED TO *KILL* HULK IS STILL ...*ALIVE!*

12

AND, INDEED, THE MANDARIN *IS* VERY MUCH ALIVE...IN ANOTHER SECTOR OF HIS CITADEL...

THUS FAR, HE EXCEEDS MY EVERY *ANTICIPATION!*

BUT, IN A GAMBIT SUCH AS MINE, I CAN TAKE NO *CHANCES!*

THE *SUPREME TRIALS* REMAIN TO BE PASSED.. AND I CANNOT ACCEPT HIM UNTIL HE HAS PASSED THEM *ALL!*

SO NOW LET US SEE HOW HE FARES AGAINST ONE EVEN *BIGGER... STRONGER* THAN HIMSELF!

THOUGH HE IS MERELY A GIGANTIC *ANDROID,* HE WILL SERVE MY PURPOSE *ADMIRABLY!*

THEN, AS THE HULK SEARCHES FOR HIS TORMENTOR IN CONFUSED *BEWILDERMENT...*

WHA--? AT *LAST!* SOMETHING *REAL...* SOMETHING HULK CAN *FIGHT!*

13

BUT, AS OUR RAGING GREEN GOLIATH GLOATS IN HIS SEEMING *TRIUMPH...*

HE IS STRONG AS *HULK!* HE GETS *UP* AGAIN!

IT IS TIME-- FOR HULK-- TO *LEAP* AGAIN--!

--BUT *NOT* AT GIANT *ENEMY*--!

THIS TIME HULK WILL DO WHAT HE DOES NOT *EXPECT*--

FIRST, I RIP *DRAPES* RIGHT OFF THE WALL--!

15

--NOBODY!

KRASH!

NOW LET THE MASKED MAN *SHOW* HIMSELF--IF HE *DARES!*

AND, INDEED, THE MANDARIN *MIGHT* HAVE SECOND THOUGHTS AS HE WATCHES THE FLIGHT OF HIS ILL-FATED GLADIATOR...

...HURTLING LIKE A *ROCKET* INTO THE DARK, COLD VOID OF *OUTER SPACE!*

LISTEN TO ME! ATTEMPT TO COMPREHEND WHAT I AM ABOUT TO *SAY!*

YOU HAVE PASSED ALL MY *TESTS*... WITHOUT THE SLIGHTEST *MISCUE!*

THEREFORE, I HAVE CHOSEN TO LET YOU BECOME...MY *ALLY!*

WHAT?!!

THE HULK SIDES WITH *NO ONE!*

CRAWSHH!

EVERYONE *HATES* HULK... AND HULK *HATES EVERYONE!*

WITH BLOWS LIKE *BULLDOZER* THRUSTS, THE RAMPAGING HULK PLOWS THROUGH WALL AND MACHINERY ALIKE, UNTIL...

MASKED MAN TRIED TO *KILL* HULK...BUT HULK WILL GET HIM *FIRST!*

17

IT IS AS I *FEARED!* THE HULK IS AS *UNCONTROLLABLE* AS HE IS STRONG!

BUT, I HAD *ANTICIPATED* AS MUCH...AND I AM *PREPARED!*

GUARDS!

PROCEED TO SECTOR Q... *IMMEDIATELY!* THE HULK MUST BE *STOPPED!*

WE HEAR... AND *OBEY,* MASTER!

MASKED MAN MUST BE *CRAZY!* AFTER HULK BEAT THE CREATURE...NOW HE SENDS PUNY *SOLDIERS* TO FACE ME!

BUT *NO* ARMY IS BIG ENOUGH TO STOP HULK!

THERE HE IS! COMMENCE FIRING ON THE BRUTE! WE MUST BRING HIM DOWN!

WE ARE *TRYING,* HONORABLE CAPTAIN ...BUT THE BULLETS MERELY *BOUNCE OFF* HIM!

THEN, AS THE TERRIFIED GUARDS LOOK ON IN *STUNNED CONFUSION*--

THESE TWO WALLS HOLD THE *ROOF* UP... SO, IF *WALLS* COLLAPSE...

18

...SO WILL ROOF!

NOW HULK MUST FIND *MASKED MAN!*

WHAT'S *LOCKED* BEHIND IRON DOOR--?

HAH! NO ONE CAN HIDE FROM HULK!

HULK WAS *RIGHT!*

MASKED MAN WAS *WAITING* FOR HULK... BUT HE WON'T WAIT ANY *LONGER!*

19

WHY DON'T YOU *MOVE?* WHY DON'T YOU TRY TO *FIGHT?*

OR ARE YOU *AFRAID* TO FACE HULK... WITHOUT HELP FROM *ROBOTS*--OR *ARMY?*

THEY CAN'T *SAVE* YOU... BECAUSE NOW... *HULK STRIKES!*

WHA...?

HULK LANDED RIGHT ON *TOP* OF YOU...BUT NOW YOU START TO *VANISH!*

AND HULK IS *FALLING* INTO SOME KIND OF *PIT*...

...FILLED WITH STICKY *MUD*-- PULLING ME *DOWN!* MUST BE--

...QUICKSAND!

VERY *PERCEPTIVE*...ESPECIALLY FOR ONE WITH SO *PRIMITIVE* A BRAIN AS *YOURS!*

YOU HAVE ONE CHANCE TO *SURVIVE,* HOWEVER! YOU NEED ONLY AGREE TO BE MY UNQUESTIONING *SLAVE*...

NEVER! HULK WOULD RATHER *DIE...*

THEN SO BE IT, YOU HELPLESS *FOOL!*

AND, AS THE MANDARIN TURNS AWAY, NOTHING REMAINS OF THE HULK SAVE A FEW LAST, DESPERATE BUBBLES ATOP THE *QUICKSAND*... A GRIM REMINDER THAT EVEN THE MOST *POWERFUL* OF BEINGS MUST SOME DAY MEET HIS *MATCH!*

CONTINUED NEXT ISSUE?

20

[143]

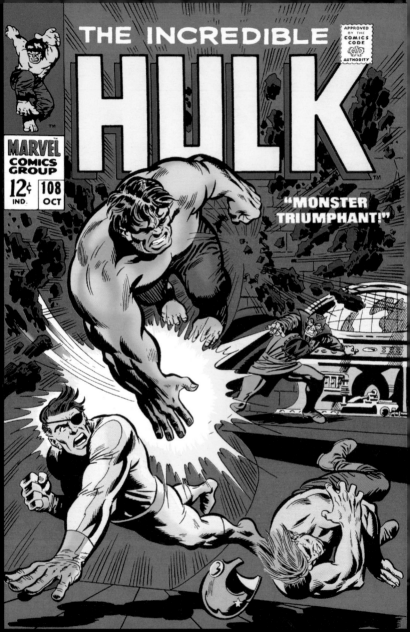

FAREWELL, MONSTER!

SUCH IS THE FATE OF *ALL* WHO ARE CALLOW ENOUGH TO DEFY--

THE MULTI-POWERED *MANDARIN!*

BUT EVEN AS THE MERCILESS ARCH-FIEND SLINKS AWAY...

HULK'S *STRENGTH* --IS *USELESS!*

CAN'T FIGHT-- STICKY *SAND*--!

SINKING DEEPER-- *DEEPER*--SAND GETTING IN NOSE --AND IN--*WAIT!*

WALL-- AT SIDE OF SAND!

HULK CAN *HIT* WALL--CAN *SMASH* IT--!

WHAT--WAS *THAT?*

HE FOUND AN *ESCAPE!*

HIS BRAIN IS *LESS BESTIAL* THAN I SUPPOSED!

NOW YOU *PAY*-- FOR TRYING TO KILL *HULK!*

PULLING THAT *LEVER*--CAN'T *HELP* YOU!

AH SO? LET US *SEE--!*

CLICK!

2

MASTER! MASTER! THE MONSTER WAKES!

KKRAK!

HE BREAKS THE GALVANIZED *CHAINS* AS THOUGH THEY ARE MERE BANDS OF *RUBBER!*

DO NOT *PANIC!*

IT WAS TO BE *EXPECTED!*

LEAVE ME, ALL! I WISH TO FACE MY GARGANTUAN SERVANT *ALONE!*

SERVANT!?? THE HULK SERVES NO ONE!

THIS TIME--YOU WON'T *ESCAPE* AGAIN!

FOOL! YOU THINK I WISH TO *ESCAPE* YOU?

PTAK!

IT IS *YOU* WHO CANNOT ESCAPE!

YOU--ARE-- *MASTER!*

I AM YOUR *MASTER!* YOU MUST DO MY *BIDDING-- FOREVER!*

ATTENTION, LAUNCH PAD! BEGIN **COUNT-DOWN** ON SUBSONIC ROCKET MZ-3!

WE WILL FACE THIS **TOGETHER,** NICK FURY!

THEN, IN A MATTER OF **MINUTES**--

WE'VE **GOT** TO FIND HIM--IN **TIME!**

BUT, THERE ARE **OTHERS** WHO HAVE THE SAME CONCERN--

DEATH TO THE ENEMIES OF THE PEOPLES' REPUBLIC!

LONG LIVE THE HONORABLE **CHAIRMAN!**

OUR WESTERN **COMRADES** HAVE SHOWN THEIR **TRUE COLORS!** THEY **ATTACK** US, EVEN **NOW!**

BUT WE SHALL **FIGHT** BACK!

EVEN **NOW,** OUR **INVINCIBLE** FORCES PROCEED TO **REPEL** THE ENEMY!

WHILE, AT THE JUBILANT *MANDARIN'S* CONTROL CENTRAL--

NOTHING CAN STOP ME *NOW!*

THE *HULK* IS WORTH A *HUNDRED DIVISIONS!*

AND HE IS *MINE* TO COMMAND!

BUT, HE MUST *LEAVE* THE TERMINAL, BEFORE HE IS *STOPPED!*

SOMETHING MAKES ME LEAP INTO *AIR* AGAIN--!

I MUST FIND *POWER PLANT--* BEYOND THE MOUNTAINS!

AND, AFTER A SWIFT SERIES OF THE GREATEST *LEAPS* EVER ATTAINED BY ANY LIVING BEING--

BUHTOOMS

TANKS COME TOWARD ME-- TO *SMASH* THE HULK!

BUT MY *STRENGTH* WILL CRUSH THEM *ALL!*

8

HULK *NEEDS* NO TANKS-- *NEEDS* NO GUNS!

THE MORE I *FIGHT*-- THE *STRONGER* I GROW!

MEANWHILE, STREAKING OVER THE DARKENING ASIAN SKIES--

HE'S NO LONGER AT THE *TERMINAL!* WE MUST SEARCH *ANEW!*

YA GOTTA *HAND* TO THAT JOKER! HE'LL TACKLE A WHOLE BLAMED *ARMY,* SINGLE-HANDED--

AND HE WON'T *STOP*--TILL HE'S *LICKED* EM TO A FRAZZLE!

BUT HE *MUST* BE STOPPED-- BEFORE HE PLUNGES THE ENTIRE *WORLD* INTO ATOMIC *WAR!*

OKAY! OKAY! BUT IF WAR *COMES,* YA CAN'T PIN IT ALL ON *HIM!* DON'T FERGET YER *OWN* POSTER-PAINTIN' LITTLE PARTNERS!

I DO NOT NEED TO BE *REMINDED,* COLONEL!

SUDDENLY, AS RAW-EDGED *TEMPERS* GROW DANGEROUSLY *TENSE*--THE IMAGE OF *TONY STARK* APPEARS ON THE ROCKET'S ALL-WAVE VIDEOCEIVER--

IF MY WORDS REACH *NICK FURY,* ANYWHERE IN THE WORLD--

THE ORDER IS-- *CODE 6!*

CODE 6! THAT STANDS FOR THE *MANDARIN!*

STARK MUSTA FIGURED OUT THAT *HE'S* BEHIND THE HULK'S RAMPAGE!

BETTER *CHANGE* YER COURSE, MISTER!

I HAVE ALREADY *DONE* SO, COLONEL--

WE WILL REACH THE MYSTERIOUS ONE'S *STRONGHOLD* IN A MATTER OF *MINUTES!*

AND, EVEN AS THE DESPERATE **MANDARIN** RECOILS IN ALARM--

WHY IS HULK **HERE** --FIGHTING UNKNOWN **TANKS?**

IT IS THE **MANDARIN**-- WHO IS HULK'S **ENEMY!**

IT IS THE **MANDARIN** I MUST FIND--AND **DESTROY!**

TANKS MOVE **BACK**--WAITING --FEARING HULK!

I FEEL SOMETHING **FALL**--FROM BACK OF MY **NECK!**

BUT, **NOTHING** MATTERS-- EXCEPT **MANDARIN!**

WHEREVER HE HIDES--HULK WILL **FIND** HIM!

HOWEVER, THE WORLD'S MOST FEARED **KARATE MASTER** IS DOING FAR **MORE** THAN MERELY HIDING--

THERE IS NO NEED TO SQUANDER THE POWER OF A **RING** ON ONE SUCH AS **YOU!**

NOW **FALL!** FALL TO YOUR **DEATH!**

TO THE **SAME** CERTAIN DEATH THAT AWAITS **ALL** MEN WHO DO NOT SERVE THE **MANDARIN!**

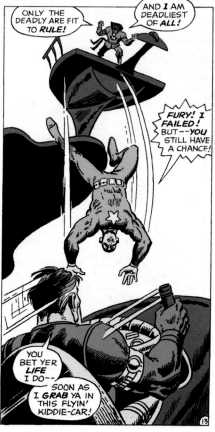

ONLY THE DEADLY ARE FIT TO **RULE!**

AND **I** AM DEADLIEST OF **ALL!**

FURY! I FAILED! BUT--**YOU** STILL HAVE A CHANCE!

YOU BET YER **LIFE** I DO-- SOON AS I **GRAB** YA IN THIS FLYIN' KIDDIE-CAR!

HOWEVER, NOT EVEN THE BATTLE-WISE *MANDARIN* IS PREPARED FOR THE BLISTERING *SPEED* OF NICK FURY'S *COUNTERATTACK*--!

THE INITIATIVE'S *OURS*, NOW, YURI--

AND WE AIN'T GONNA *BLOW* IT!

THIS *GRENADE BLAST* OUGHTTA KNOCK 'IM OFFA HIS CRUMMY *PERCH*!

GOOD *SHOT*, FURY!

BLAST IT! LOOKS LIKE *HE* CAN SAVE HIMSELF FROM A FALL--SAME AS *US*!

DA! --THRU THE POWER OF HIS UNCANNY *ENERGY RINGS*!

SO *WHAT*? WE *STILL* GOT 'IM ON THE *RUN*, DON'T WE?

I--AM NOT *CERTAIN*, COLONEL!

FOR *THAT* YOU SHALL PAY--*MOST DEARLY*!

A *PITY* YOU CANNOT SQUEEZE YOUR TRIGGER FINGERS AS FAST AS *I* CAN ACTIVATE MY *RINGS*!

NOW IT IS *TOO LATE*! MY *STUN GAS* WORKS-- *INSTANTLY*!

WOULD THAT I HAD BEEN ABLE TO *DEFEAT* THE *HULK*--AS EASILY!

BUT, EVEN AS THE FIGHTING RAMROD OF *SHIELD* BEGINS TO TOTTER...

I *LAUGHED* AT STARK WHEN HE SHOVED THIS *MINI-MASK* IN MY HOLSTER!

BUT I SURE AIN'T LAUGHIN' *NOW!*

YURI'S *DOWN!* SO IT'S UP TA *ME!* WHEN THE SMOKE *CLEARS,* HE'LL EXPECT'A FIND US *BOTH* OUTTA ACTION--!

THIS IS *IT!*

AWRIGHT, CRUM-BUM-- HERE'S WHERE I SEE WHAT MAKES YA *TICK!*

I SUGGEST YOU DO NOTHING *RASH,* DOOMED ONE--

NOT UNTIL YOU LOOK *ABOVE* YOU--!

I AM WELL *AWARE* OF THE GREAT *VALUE* YOU AMERICANS PUT UPON HUMAN *LIFE!*

A VALUE WHICH SHALL INSURE MY *VICTORY!*

SOME KINDA DEADLY *GIZMO*-- AIMED AT *BREVLOV!*

SHOULD YOU *FIRE* YOUR HAND-HELD *GRENADE LAUNCHER* AT ME, THE VERY *SOUND* OF ITS BLAST WILL ACTIVATE THE *LASER RAY* WHICH IS BEAMED UPON YOUR HELPLESS ALLY!

CAN'T LET 'IM MURDER YURI-- BUT, IF I GIVE IN, WE'RE *BOTH* DONE FOR!

THUS, I ORDER YOU TO *DROP* YOUR NOW-USELESS WEAPON--AT *ONCE!*

16

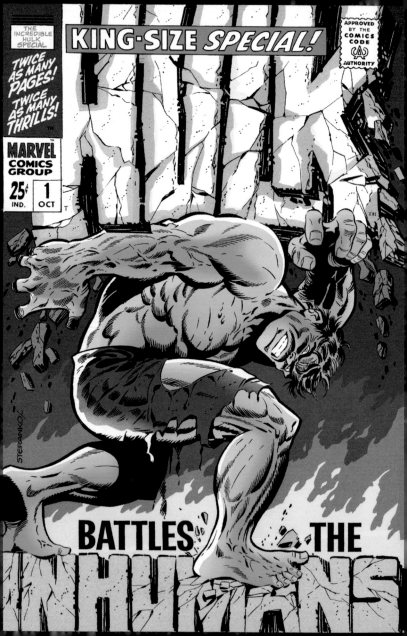

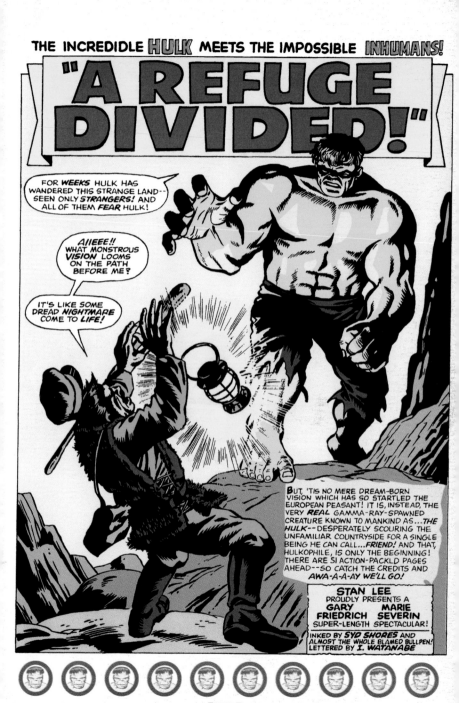

BUT, WHILE THE TORMENTED GREEN GOLIATH PONDERS HIS LONELY FATE, EVENTS ARE SHAPING BUT A FEW MILES AWAY WHICH ARE DESTINED TO ALTER THE COURSE OF THE HULK'S *DESTINY*...

...FOR, AT THAT VERY INSTANT, A LONE, SILENT FIGURE SWOOPS TOWARD A GLEAMING CITY HIDDEN DEEP WITHIN THE BOWELS OF THE *ALPS*--ON A MISSION OF SUCH GRAVE IMPORTANCE THAT THE FATE OF AN ENTIRE *RACE* HANGS IN THE BALANCE, AWAITING HIS *ARRIVAL*...

HEAR ME, O CITIZENS OF THIS *GREAT REFUGE!* OUR SUMMONS HAS BEEN HEARD AND ANSWERED BY OUR SUPREME SOVEREIGN...

BLACK BOLT!

FROM *FAR-OFF LANDS* HAS HE COME, TO STAND IN REGAL *JUDGMENT* IN THE DEEP MATTER BEFORE US!

...SO NOW I PASS UNTO HIM THE HOLY *SCEPTRE OF JUSTICE* --TO GUIDE HIM IN THIS ALL-IMPORTANT DECISION!

AND NOW, LET THE *ACCUSED* BE BROUGHT FORTH!

3

THEN, AS THE GREAT DOG, LOCK-JAW, WHISKS THE CONVICTS TO THEIR APPOINTED SPHERE OF EXILE AT A SPEED FAR FASTER THAN THAT OF *LIGHT*...

...AN ANGRY, FRIGHTENED *MOB* COMBS THE HILLS NEAR THE GREAT REFUGE --IN SEARCH OF THE *HULK*...

IT WAS NEAR THIS *PASS* THAT I SAW THE MONSTER!

HARD TO BELIEVE THOUGH IT MAY BE... IT IS *POSSIBLE*...

...FOR, ACCORDING TO OUR *ANCESTORS*, MANY SIGHTS FAR STRANGER THAN *FICTION* HAVE BEEN SEEN IN THIS AREA!

SUDDENLY--

EEYAAAA! A GIGANTIC DOG... A *DEVIL-HOUND*! QUICK... THE *TORCHES* WILL FRIGHTEN IT!

SO, PUNY VILLAGERS DARE TO *HUNT* HULK... AND BRING BIG DOG TO *HELP* THEM! IF IT'S *BATTLE* THEY WANT... HULK WILL *GIVE* IT TO THEM!

THEN, AS THE STARTLED LOCKJAW TURNS TO *FACE* HIM WHO HAS JUST SPOKEN, HIS ONLY THOUGHTS ARE TO DO THAT WHICH HE HAS BEEN SO PAINSTAKINGLY TRAINED TO DO... PROTECT THE GREAT REFUGE FROM DISCOVERY BY ALL *STRANGERS*...

HULK NEVER *SAW* SUCH A HUGE DOG BEFORE... BUT IT ISN'T BIG ENOUGH TO HURT *ME*!

EYOWRR!

NOTHING CAN HURT HULK... AND NOW HULK WILL PROVE IT!

WAIT--DOG ATTACKS--!

DOG IS HEAVIER... *STRONGER* THAN HULK THOUGHT! HULK WILL NEED ALL HIS STRENGTH ... TO BEAT IT!

BUT... ₹UUNNNHHH ₹... HULK **WILL** WIN!

GROWRR!

However, as the Hulk is about to hurl his canine adversary against the jagged **MOUNTAINSIDE**...

WHAT IS **HAPPENING?**

FEEL STRANGE...AS IF **FLYING THRU SPACE**...!

AND, THOUGH THE GREAT GREEN GARGOYLE CAN HARDLY COMPREHEND WHAT IS TAKING **PLACE**...

HULK BEING **PULLED** SOMEWHERE...BY SOME NEW, POWERFUL **FORCE!** BUT **WHERE**...**HOW?**

...IT SHOULD BE QUITE CLEAR TO ALL INHUMANS-IDOLIZERS THAT LOCKJAW, IN SELF-DEFENSE, HAS ONCE MORE BROUGHT INTO PLAY HIS **INTER-DIMENSIONAL TELEPORTATION POWERS**...

ALTHOUGH NOT WITH THE MOST **SUCCESSFUL** OF RESULTS...

HULK DOESN'T **CARE** WHERE HE'S GOING!

ALL THAT MATTERS IS THAT DOG IS **BEATEN** ...HERE AND **NOW!**

SO, HAVING FAILED TO **STARTLE** THE HULK INTO RELEASING HIS IRON-HARD GRIP, LOCKJAW INSTANTANEOUSLY RETURNS TO **EARTH**...

BA WUMMP!

10

AND, AS THE HULK DESPERATELY TRIES TO SHATTER THE ALL-CONFINING *BARRIER*, THE EYES OF YET ONE *MORE* INHUMAN ARE UPON HIM...

THE INTER-DIMENSIONAL VIEWER I CONSTRUCTED IS A *SUCCESS!* I HAVE TUNED IN THE *BANISHED ONES!*

...BUT, WHO IS THE MONSTROUS CREATURE *WITH* THEM...WHO IS TRYING TO SHATTER THE IMPRISONING *FORCE FIELD?*

HE CANNOT BE ONE OF *US*...FOR MAXIMUS KNOWS *ALL* WHO DWELL WITHIN THIS REFUGE!

YET, IF HE WAS NOT SENT TO THE *UN-PLACE* BY BLACK BOLT, HOW *DID* HE GET THERE?

NO MATTER! HE SEEMS SO POWERFUL... PERHAPS HIS MINDLESS *MIGHT* CAN AID ME IN WHAT I DESIRE TO *DO--!*

YOU *FAILED*, MONSTROUS ONE... JUST AS WE *PREDICTED!* NOW PERHAPS YOU WILL *SWALLOW* YOUR STUPID PRIDE...AND *ACCEPT* YOUR FATE!

HE MIGHT AS *WELL!* FOR, LIKE ME, HE IS TRAPPED HERE FOR *ETERNITY!*

NO! GIVING UP IS FOR *COWARDS*... NOT FOR... THE HULK!

HULK WILL TRY *AGAIN*... AND AGAIN... UNTIL INVISIBLE WALL *BREAKS!*

KWOOMM!

13

AHH, BUT YOU ARE *WRONG!*

THERE COMES A DAY WHEN *EVERY* MAN MUST HAVE AT LEAST ONE HE CAN CALL *FRIEND!*

HORSEMAN *LIES!* HULK HAS *NEVER* HAD FRIEND!

THEN, WHAT BETTER TIME TO START *BUILDING* FRIENDSHIPS --THAN *NOW?*

AND, I WARN YOU--TO *REFUSE* OUR HOSPITALITY COULD BE MOST *UNCOMFORTABLE* FOR YOU!

THEN, WITH BUT THE SLIGHTEST GESTURE OF HIS FINGER, THE TREE-DWELLER CAUSES ALL NEARBY PLANTS TO SUDDENLY SPRING TO *LIFE...*

GRASS SHOOTING UP ALL *AROUND* ME... *ATTACKING* ME!

BUT NOTHING...NOT EVEN *MAGIC TRICKS*...CAN MAKE HULK DO WHAT HE DOESN'T WANT TO DO!

NOW HULK WILL SHOW TREE-MAN HOW TO STOP MAGIC...WITH *STRENGTH!*

BY THE GODS OF ALL THAT GROWS! HE'S UPROOTED THE VERY GROUND I WAS STANDING ON.!..

...AS IF IT WERE BUT A MERE PEBBLE!

THIS WILL SHOW THEM THAT NO ONE THREATENS HULK!

WHROOM!

NOW MAYBE TREE-MAN WILL BELIEVE WHEN HULK SAYS HE DOESN'T WANT TO JOIN ANY-BODY!

SO GROGGY... EVERYTHING SPINNING...

...BUT, NOTHING SEEMS TO BE BROKEN!

AND AT LEAST I HAVE LEARNED THAT MY POWERS ...PERHAPS ALL OF OUR POWERS COMBINED...ARE NO MATCH FOR THOSE OF THE GREEN-SKINNED GIANT WHO HAS BEEN THRUST INTO OUR MIDST!

SUDDENLY...

HULK HAS MADE HIS POINT! NOW MAYBE STRANGE ONES WILL LEAVE ME ALONE--AND...

WHA--?

BRIGHT LIGHT... FILLING AIR... BLINDING HULK!

MAYBE ANOTHER OF THEM IS GOING TO ATTACK ME!

17

BUT, AS THE STARTLED GARGANTUA BRACES FOR ANOTHER *ONSLAUGHT*...

HOLD YOUR *TEMPER*, BRUTE! DO NOT LASH OUT SIMPLY BECAUSE YOU DO NOT UNDERSTAND!

I COME AS *FRIEND*...NOT AS *FOE*-- AND I WILL *DELIVER* YOU FROM THIS PLACE!

YOU NEED ONLY AGREE TO BECOME MY *ALLIES*--HELP ME REGAIN MY RIGHTFUL *THRONE*...TO GAIN EVER-LASTING *PEACE*...AND *FRIENDSHIP*!

IT IS *MAXIMUS*... BUT HOW DID HE GET HERE?

THAT MATTERS *NOT*! HE OBVIOUSLY INTENDS TO RETURN US TO THE *REFUGE*!

PRECISELY, STALLIOR-- FOR, WITH MY HELP, YOU MAY *STILL* ACHIEVE YOUR GOAL OF OVER-THROWING *BLACK BOLT*!

I HAVE PERFECTED AN INTER-DIMENSIONAL *TELEPORTER*-- WITH POWERS THAT EQUAL THOSE OF *LOCKJAW*, HIMSELF! AND, WITH IT, I SHALL RETURN YOU ALL TO THE HOME FROM WHICH YOU WERE *BANISHED*!

THEN, WITH THE HELP OF HE WHO CALLS HIMSELF *HULK*...RULE OF THE GREAT REFUGE WILL BE *OURS*!

SO, *BRACE* YOURSELVES! WITHIN BUT A MICROSECOND ...WE WILL BE *HOME*!

NO! HULK WON'T *GO* WITH YOU! HULK DOESN'T *TRUST* YOU!

NO ONE FORCES HULK TO...

HE *FADED* AWAY...

...AND NOW, HULK IS FADING *TOO*!

18

HOWEVER, AS MAXIMUS AND HIS FOLLOWERS RUSH TOWARD AN *ESCAPE EXIT*...

HULK *WON'T RUN!* HULK IS NOT AFRAID OF PUNY GUARDS... OR THEIR *RAY GUNS!* HULK WILL *STOP* THEM ...CRUSH THEM ALL!

IT ISN'T MAXIMUS *AFTER ALL*...BUT IT MAY BE EVEN *WORSE!* OUR *DISINTEGRATORS* DON'T HAVE ANY *EFFECT* ON THAT MONSTER!

HAH! NOW YOU KNOW GUNS WON'T HURT HULK--BUT YOU FOUND OUT TOO *LATE!*--HULK DIDN'T *ASK* FOR TROUBLE--BUT, SINCE YOU *GAVE* IT TO ME, HULK WILL SHOW YOU WHAT TROUBLE *MEANS!*

AND, WHILE OL' GREEN-SKIN IS MOPPING UP THE LABORATORY WITH THE REFUGE'S *ELITE GUARD*...

HURRY, MAXIMUS! NOT EVEN THE HULK CAN HOLD THE GUARD FOR-EVER--AND, IF WE SHOULD BE *CAPTURED*...

...THE ONLY POSSIBLE PUNISHMENT REMAINING FOR US WOULD CERTAINLY BE...*DEATH!*

SILENCE, YOU SPINELESS COWARD! ALL IS IN *READINESS!* FOLLOW ME INTO THE CAPSULE WHICH LIES JUST BEYOND THIS *PANEL!*

THEN, SECONDS LATER...

I CONSTRUCTED THIS EMERGENCY VORTEX-ELEVATOR MANY *YEARS* AGO--BEFORE BLACK BOLT FORBADE ME TO EVER *ENTER* THE LABORATORY AGAIN...

...KNOWING FULL-WELL THAT I WOULD ONE DAY *RETURN*--AND MIGHT HAVE DIRE *NEED* OF IT!

20

BUT, SINCE WE KNOW HOW BORED YOU CAN GET LISTENING TO A MADMAN RANT AND RAVE--SUPPOSING WE SEE HOW THE *INHUMANS' LAW ENFORCEMENT* CENTER IS HOLDING UP...

WE WILL DISPATCH *PATROL ATTACK CRAFT* TO THE AREA...WITH ORDERS TO SHOOT THE CREATURE ON *SIGHT!*

OUR SENTINELS DIDN'T HAVE A *CHANCE* AGAINST THE MONSTER! WHAT WILL WE DO *NOW?* HE MUST BE *STOPPED!*

AS YOU WISH, SIR! *ATTENTION PATROL ATTACK CRAFT DIVISION*--DISPATCH ALL AIRBORNE CRAFT TO SECTOR-H IMMEDIATELY!

AN UNKNOWN ALIEN HAS BROKEN INTO THE FORBIDDEN LABORATORY OF *MAXIMUS!* HE MUST BE *DESTROYED!*

PATROL ATTACK NUMBER 743 TO HEADQUARTERS! TARGET SPOTTED! WILL AWAIT *REINFORCEMENTS* BEFORE ATTACKING!

BUT, HULK DOESN'T CARE-- AS LONG AS HE CAN LEAVE THEM ALL *BEHIND...*

MAYBE EVEN LEAVE THE WHOLE *WORLD* BEHIND!

HOWEVER, AS THE HULK HURTLES HIGH ABOVE THE GLISTENING SPIRES OF THE GREAT REFUGE--SO LOST IN HIS THOUGHTS IS HE THAT HE IS *OBLIVIOUS* TO THE DEADLY AIRCRAFT BEARING DOWN *BEHIND* HIM...

NOW THAT GUARDS HAVE FLED...HULK CAN *LEAP AWAY* FROM THIS PLACE!

PEOPLE HERE ARE EVEN MORE *MADDENING* THAN *NORMAL MEN* WHO HUNT AND HOUND HULK!

UNTIL...

ZAK

UNNNH!

21

PLANES *BACK OFF* NOW! THEY'RE AFRAID TO ATTACK HULK ANY MORE!

BUT THEY KEEP CIRCLING *OVERHEAD!* WON'T LET HULK *ESCAPE* BY LEAPING!

SO, HULK WILL HAVE TO *SMASH* HIS WAY THROUGH THE CITY...

...AND OVER ANYONE WHO GETS IN MY *WAY!*

BUT, NOW THAT IT'S BEEN MADE CLEAR TO US WHAT *HULKY'S* GONNA BE UP TO FOR THE NEXT FEW PAGES...

...LET'S SEE WHAT'S SHAKIN' WITH *MAXIMUS*...

WHERE ARE YOU *TAKING* US, MAXIMUS? IT SEEMS WE HAVE BEEN WALKING THROUGH THIS MAZE OF MACHINERY FOR *HOURS!*

YOU WILL SOON *SEE,* MY FRIENDS––BUT, BEFORE WE REACH OUR DESTINATION...

...LET ME FIRST EXPLAIN THAT WHICH YOU ARE ABOUT TO *WITNESS!*

IN ANCIENT TIMES, *CENTURIES* BEFORE OUR GENERATION'S BIRTH, A SCIENTIST NAMED *ROMNAR* CONDUCTED SOME....*INTERESTING* EXPERIMENTS!

WE DO NOT NEED A *HISTORY LESSON,* MAXIMUS! WE WANT THE *THRONE!*

PATIENCE, LEONUS! PATIENCE!

SO DANGEROUS––AND SO *DEADLY* WERE ROMNAR'S EXPERIMENTS ––THAT HE WAS EVENTUALLY *ARRESTED*––BUT HE LEFT BEHIND SOMETHING HIS CAPTORS WERE NOT PREPARED TO *COPE* WITH...

DON'T *TOUCH* THAT, YOU FOOLS! YOUR WITLESS BUMBLINGS COULD WELL DESTROY THE ENTIRE *WORLD!*

TAKE HIM *AWAY!* HE IS MERELY AFRAID WE WILL DISCOVER HIS *SECRETS!*

AND, INDEED THE GOVERNMENT *DID* LEARN THE DREAD *SECRET* OF ROMNAR'S WORKS... BUT NOT IN THE WAY IT HAD *ANTICIPATED*

23

FIRST, THE STRANGE, GLOWING SUBSTANCE ROMNAR HAD CREATED ABSORBED *ONE MAN*...THEN ANOTHER...AND ANOTHER--ALL THE WHILE GAINING EVERY IOTA OF ENERGY WITHIN WHATEVER IT *ABSORBED!* AND AFTER BUT A FEW HOURS...

RUN FOR YOUR LIVES! *IT* IS COMING!

IF WE STAY HERE...*IT* WILL DEVOUR US ALL!

HOWEVER, IN TIME, AND AFTER THOUSANDS OF *LIVES* HAD BEEN LOST, THE SUBSTANCE WAS *SUBDUED*...

IT IS *BEATEN!* WE HAVE FINALLY *WON!*

BUT IT IS NOT *DEAD!* WE HAVE SUCCEEDED ONLY IN *CONTROLLING* IT! NOW, A PLACE MUST BE FOUND TO *IMPRISON* IT...*FOREVER!*

AND, INDEED, SUCH A PLACE WAS *BUILT*...

WITHIN THESE VERY *WALLS* THE SECRET SUBSTANCE NOW LIES-- WAITING TO ONCE MORE BE *UNLEASHED!*

AND MAXIMUS HAS IT WITHIN HIS POWER TO SET IT *FREE*...AND TO MAKE IT *OBEDIENT!*

IN OTHER WORDS, BEHIND THIS WALL LIES THE *ULTIMATE WEAPON*-- WHICH WE SHALL EMPLOY TO BRING BLACK BOLT TO HIS *KNEES*...

AND TO BRING TO OURSELVES THE POWER AND THE GLORY WE RIGHT-FULLY *DESERVE!*

24

BUT, IF THIS SUBSTANCE IS SO *ALL-POWERFUL*, WHY HAVE YOU WAITED UNTIL NOW TO *OBTAIN* IT?

AND, WITH YOUR GREAT SCIENTIFIC GENIUS, WHY DO YOU NEED *US*?

BECAUSE THIS WALL WHICH *HOLDS* THE SUBSTANCE CANNOT BE *PENETRATED* BY ANYTHING MECHANICAL!

FOR *YEARS* I HAVE BEEN TRYING--BUT ALWAYS I HAVE *FAILED*!

UNTIL, RECENTLY, I FINALLY DISCOVERED ITS *SECRET*...IT CAN ONLY BE PENETRATED BY SHEER, *LIVING ENERGY*!

IF THE SOURCE OF SUCH ENERGY IS *POWERFUL* ENOUGH...THE WALL WILL *ABSORB* IT...

THE FIRST STEP IS TO *FIND* THAT CREATURE...AND SOMEHOW CONVINCE HIM TO *ASSIST* US--AND THAT TASK CAN ONLY FALL TO *NEBULO,* THE SHADOW!

VERY WELL, MAXIMUS! I WILL *LOCATE* HIM FOR YOU--BUT ONLY ON YOUR PROMISE THAT I WILL ONE DAY BE YOUR *SECOND IN COMMAND!*

...AND THAT IS WHERE YOU, AND THE *GREEN-HUED ONE,* FIT INTO MY PLANS!

WHAT? WHY SHOULD *YOU* BE MADE... ≷UUNNNHHH≷

I ASSUME THIS IS *SUFFICIENT ANSWER,* COWARD!

HALT! I COMMAND YOU TO CEASE THESE USELESS HOSTILITIES AT ONCE! HOW CAN WE HOPE TO DEFEAT A *COMMON ENEMY*--WHEN WE ARE ENEMIES UNTO EACH OTHER?

TOGETHER, WE CAN RULE FIRST THE *REFUGE*...THEN THE WORLD...AND ONE DAY THE *UNIVERSE*...

BUT, DIVIDED, WE CAN RULE ONLY OUR- SELVES...IN *EXILE!*

25

MAXIMUS SPEAKS WORDS OF *WISDOM*...AND NEBULO WILL RESPOND TO HIS WISHES! I NOW WILL DEPART TO FIND THE *HULK*...PROVIDED, OF COURSE, MAXIMUS AGREES TO MY *DEMAND!*

BUT OF *COURSE!* YOU HAVE ONLY TO PROVE YOUR WORTH ON THIS MISSION--TO ONE DAY SIT AT MY *RIGHT* ON THE THRONE!

NOW, GO FORTH AND *FIND* THIS HULK...AND, SOMEHOW, BRING HIM *HERE!*

THE FATE OF US *ALL* RESTS ON YOUR *SHOULDERS!*

THEN, WITHIN MERE MOMENTS, THE MAN WHO IS BUT A SHADOW SLIPS UNNOTICED THROUGH THE HEAVILY-GUARDED STREETS, *UNTIL...*

A *SPECIAL SENTRY* ...PRECISELY WHAT I HAVE BEEN *SEEKING!*

I NEED ONLY RENDER HIM *UNCONSCIOUS* TO LEARN THE WHEREABOUTS OF MY *QUARRY!*

AND, AS THE SPECIAL SENTINEL OF BLACK BOLT STOPS TO *REST...*

HE IS SWIFTLY STRUCK DOWN FROM *BEHIND...*

...BY AN INVISIBLE ENEMY!

STEP ONE OF MY MISSION *GOES WELL!*

NOW I MUST DRAG HIM INTO AN *ALLEY* WHERE HE WILL NOT SOON BE *DISCOVERED!*

AND NOW, MERELY BY PUTTING ON HIS *TRANS-MITTING HELMET...*

...I CAN *EASILY* FIND OUT WHERE THE HULK CAN BE *LOCATED!*

YES...HEADQUARTERS IS NOW ANNOUNCING HE IS IN *SECTOR 713!* SO I MUST GO THERE *IMMEDIATELY!*

26

THEN, AS NEBULO ARRIVES AT THE GIVEN **SECTOR**, THE EXPLOSIVE SCENE OF CARNAGE AND DESTRUCTION CAN LEAVE LITTLE **DOUBT** IN HIS MIND BUT THAT THE **CAUSE** OF IT MUST BE THE ONE HE **SEEKS**...

THIS IS BEYOND **BELIEF!** THE AIR FORCE IS DESTROYING AN ENTIRE **BLOCK**...

...IN AN ATTEMPT TO KILL ONE MERE **BEING!**

I CAN ONLY HOPE THE HULK IS CAPABLE OF **SURVIVING** SUCH AN ONSLAUGHT...AT LEAST UNTIL I CAN **REACH** HIM!

BUT, THE SHADOW-MAN WOULD BE FAR LESS **CONCERNED** IF HE COULD BUT SEE THE GREAT GREEN GOLIATH IN **ACTION** AT THAT VERY MOMENT...

PLANES KEEP **ATTACKING** HULK... BLOCKING MY PATH **OUT** OF THIS PLACE!

BUT IT WON'T DO THEM ANY **GOOD**-- BECAUSE HULK WILL SMASH THE WHOLE **WORLD** IF HE HAS TO!

AND, AS THE HULK FLEXES HIS MIGHTY MUSCLES AND GIVES A GREAT THRUST **UPWARD**...

NOW HULK WILL MAKE HIS **OWN PATH**... BY SMASHING EVERY BUILDING IN MY **WAY!**

27

EXCELLENT! YOU WILL NEVER *REGRET* IT!

IF THEY ARE *YOUR* FRIENDS...THEN THEY'LL BE *HULK'S* FRIENDS!

NOW JUST FOLLOW ME INTO THIS *TUBE!* IT LEADS TO THE UNDERGROUND HEADQUARTERS OF MY *ALLIES!*

BUT, HULK DOESN'T *UNDERSTAND* THIS STRANGE PLACE...NEVER *SAW* SO MANY MACHINES!

I REALIZE IT'S ALL DIFFICULT FOR YOU TO *COMPREHEND*... BUT JUST *TRUST* ME!

NOTHING HERE WILL *HARM* YOU...INCLUDING THE *OTHERS* WHOM WE ARE ABOUT TO *MEET!*

THEN...

LOOK! NEBULO *SUCCEEDED!* HE HAS RETURNED WITH THE ONE CALLED *HULK!*

TRUE...BUT HOW DO WE KNOW WE CAN *TRUST* THE CREATURE? HE MAY *ATTACK* US AGAIN!

THAT IS A RISK WE WILL HAVE TO *RUN*, TIMBERIUS...FOR OUR CAUSE HAS NO OTHER *HOPE!*

WELCOME! WE ARE DELIGHTED YOU HAVE DECIDED TO *JOIN* US!

HULK JOINS *NO ONE!* HULK ONLY WANTS TO *ESCAPE* FROM THIS PLACE!

AHH, BUT OF *COURSE* YOU DO...AND WE WILL *HELP* YOU...FOR WE UNDERSTAND YOUR PLIGHT!

FOR WE, LIKE YOURSELF, ARE ALL *OUTCASTS*... HATED AND HOUNDED BY ALL OTHER MEN!

WE ONLY WANT TO OFFER YOU OUR *FRIENDSHIP*... AND HOPE THAT YOU WILL GIVE US *YOURS!*

NO ONE EVER *ASKED* HULK TO BE HIS FRIEND BEFORE! NO ONE EVER *UNDERSTOOD*... BUT HULK CAN TELL YOU *DO* UNDERSTAND!

AND HULK *WILL* BE YOUR FRIEND!

29

THEN, AFTER THE HULK HAS CAREFULLY PLACED THE CUMBERSOME CONTAINER ACCORDING TO THE INSTRUCTIONS OF *MAXIMUS*...

THERE! NOW ALL IS IN READINESS FOR THE MAJOR *TEST!*

IF IT IS *SUCCESSFUL*... WE WILL BE READY TO DEMAND *FULL CONTROL* OF THE GREAT REFUGE!

YOU *ARE* SAFE! YOU'RE MY *FRIENDS!* HULK WILL PROTECT YOU!

THOUGH I FEAR NOTHING *MYSELF*, I WONDER...WOULD IT NOT BE BEST TO SEND THE OTHERS TO A PLACE OF *SAFETY?*

RIGHT! NOW STAND BACK AND WATCH! I NEED ONLY MANIPULATE THIS *LEVER*...

LOOK OUT! IT'S STARTING TO *GLOW*...AND *TREMBLE!* WE'RE ALL GOING TO BE *KILLED!*

ON THE *CONTRARY!* MY FINDINGS ARE *CONFIRMED!* I CAN CONTROL THE FORBIDDEN SUBSTANCE!

THEN, IF THAT IS SO, WHAT FURTHER NEED DO WE HAVE FOR *HIM!* I DO NOT *TRUST* HIM!

HOWEVER, WE'LL HAVE TO WAIT UNTIL *LATER* FOR MAXIMUS' *ANSWER!* FOR, AT THAT SAME MOMENT, IN THE VERY *HEART* OF THE REFUGE...

LEGIONS...IN THE ABSENCE OF BLACK BOLT ...*GORGON* DEMANDS THAT YOU *TELL* WHERE THE HULK HAS GONE!

ALAS, GORGON... I AM BUT OUR RULER'S *ORACLE!* I HAVE NO *ANSWER* FOR YOU!

BUT... *HEAR ME*, CITIZENS OF THE GREAT REFUGE! I, *MAXIMUS*, WISH TO ANNOUNCE THAT, ON THIS DAY, YOU ONCE MORE SHALL PROCLAIM ME...*KING!*

FOR I HAVE OBTAINED THE FORBIDDEN SUBSTANCE OF *RAMNOR*...AND, UNLESS THE THRONE IS SURRENDERED TO ME *IMMEDIATELY*, I SHALL UNLEASH IT UPON YOU ALL!

32

RAMNOR...THE ANCIENT CHEMIST WHO NEARLY *DESTROYED* THE REFUGE! IF MAXIMUS SPEAKS THE TRUTH...WE MAY BE *DOOMED!*

AND, A SPLIT-SECOND *LATER*, JUST OUTSIDE THE OFFICE IN WHICH GORGON AND THE ORACLE *STAND*...

LOOK! HOVERING OVER THE CITY...A BLINDING CIRCLE OF *LIGHT!*

IT IS A HALO OF *DEATH!* MAXIMUS TRULY INTENDS TO *KILL* US ALL!

RUN FOR YOUR LIVES! THE END IS NEAR!

WHILE...

MAXIMUS APPEARS TO BE BROADCASTING FROM THE *ARENA OF JUSTICE!*

I MUST *GO* THERE... AND TRY TO *STOP* HIM!

THOUGH YOU HAVE LITTLE *CHANCE*...PERHAPS YOU CAN AT LEAST *DELAY* HIM...

...WHILE I ATTEMPT TO SUMMON *BLACK BOLT!*

THEN, AS GORGON DESPERATELY FIGHTS HIS WAY THROUGH THE PANICKING THRONGS IN THE *STREETS*...

HEAR ME, CITIZENS! YOU NEED NOT FLEE IN TERROR! YOU CAN STILL BE *SPARED!*

YOU NEED ONLY TURN TO ME...AND RECOGNIZE ME AS YOUR *KING!*

PLACE ME ON THE THRONE WHICH WAS UNRIGHTFULLY USURPED FROM ME BY *BLACK BOLT*...AND I WILL SPARE YOUR LIVES!

HE HAS BECOME *CRAZED* WITH POWER... AND FORGOTTEN THAT WE *EXIST!*

IF NECESSARY, HE WILL DESTROY *US* ALONG WITH EVERYONE *ELSE!*

YOUR WORDS HAVE THE RING OF *WISDOM,* LEONUS, BUT WHAT CAN WE *DO?*

BUT, BEFORE THE LION-MAN CAN *ANSWER*...

HOLD YOUR *TONGUE,* MAXIMUS! GORGON WOULD HAVE *WORDS* WITH YOU...IN THE NAME OF OUR TRUE LEADER!

SURELY YOU DO NOT THINK YOUR MAD SCHEME CAN RETURN YOUR *THRONE* TO YOU!

AT THIS VERY MOMENT, *BLACK BOLT* IS ON HIS WAY TO *STOP* YOU!

SPEAK NOT TO ME OF MY THRONE-THIEVING *BROTHER!*

I HAVE HARNESSED ALL THE POWER OF ROMNAR'S SUBSTANCE IN THIS TINY *WRIST RAY*...AND IT IS FAR MORE THAN ENOUGH POWER TO SMITE DOWN THE LIKES OF YOU...*OR* BLACK BOLT!

NO! YOU'RE CRAZED WITH POWER, MAXIMUS! YOU'LL SLAY *EVERYONE!*

(33)

THEN...

KA-THO-OOM!

THAT IS THE END OF *ONE* OF OUR FOES...NOW, WHAT SHALL WE DO WITH THE *OTHER?*

YOU TREACHEROUS *MORONS!* CAN YOU NOT SEE THAT, WITH-OUT *ME*, YOU WILL ONLY *DESTROY* YOURSELVES?

ONLY *I* HAVE THE KNOWLEDGE TO *CONTROL* ROMNAR'S SUB-STANCE! IN THE HANDS OF ANYONE ELSE...IT COULD WELL DESTROY THIS ENTIRE *PLANET!*

YOU'RE NOT SPEAKING TO THE IGNORANT *MASSES*, MAXIMUS! YOU WON'T TRICK US INTO *SPARING*... WHA...?

THAT *LIGHT!* THE GUN WAS FORCED FROM MY *GRASP*...

THE BLINDING *GLOW* EMANATES FROM A TOWERING FIGURE ALMOST TREMBLING IN *RAGE*...

BLACK BOLT!

35

AND, WHILE THE CROWD STARES IN SHELL-SHOCKED AWE AT THE CONFRONTATION ABOUT TO TAKE PLACE ON THE BALCONY *ABOVE*...

NOW HULK *KNOWS* THEY WEREN'T MY FRIENDS!

THEY'RE LIKE ALL *OTHER* PEOPLE! THEY FEAR HULK ...*HATE* HULK! ONLY WANTED TO *USE* HULK!

BUT, SOON, HULK WILL GET HIS *REVENGE!*

BLACK BOLT COMMANDS THAT ALL THOSE WHO WERE BANISHED AND RETURNED BE *ARRESTED!*

YOU HAVE *HEARD* BLACK BOLT! *SEIZE THEM* AT ONCE!

WE ARE *SAVED!* MAXIMUS FEARS TO *ACT* AGAINST BLACK BOLT!

AND NOW OUR RULER, FOR THE FIRST TIME, *LASHES OUT* AT HIM HE MUST CLAIM AS *BROTHER!*

FOR, THIS ACT OF TREASON HAS *SURELY* BEEN THE GRAVEST OF THEM *ALL!*

THEN, MAXIMUS HAVING BEEN BRUSHED ASIDE, BLACK BOLT GESTURES DRAMATICALLY TO THE EVER-LOYAL *GORGON*...

HIS HIGHNESS WISHES THAT THE TRAITORS BE TAKEN TO *PRISON* TO AWAIT RE-SENTENCING!

IT SHALL BE DONE!

BUT, AS THE GUARDS BEGIN TO MARCH THE EVIL INHUMANS OFF--AND BLACK BOLT SOARS AWAY WITH *MAXIMUS*...

THEY TRY TO *LEAVE* WITH THOSE WHO LIED TO HULK! BUT HULK WON'T *LET* THEM!

THEY *TRICKED* HULK... MADE ME THINK THEY WERE *FRIENDS*...AND THEN *BETRAYED* ME! BUT THEY WON'T GET AWAY WITH IT! NOW...

36

HULK ATTACKS!

THE GIANT *LIVES*... AND LEAPS FORWARD TO *SLAY* US!

YOU MADE *FOOL* OF HULK... AND NOW YOU'LL *PAY* FOR IT!

WHAT CAN WE *DO?* THE GUARDS WILL NEVER BE ABLE TO *STOP* HIM!

THE CREATURE IS STILL ALIVE... BUT, *GOOD!* LET HIM HAVE HIS *MOMENT*... AND PERHAPS THEY WILL DESTROY *EACH OTHER!*

SINCE WE WILL BE SENTENCED TO DEATH, *NO MATTER*... LET US DIE LIKE *WARRIORS BORN!*

AND LET ALL KNOW THAT EVERY BLOW STRUCK BY *STALLIOR*...IS A BLOW FOR OUR *RIGHTFUL* KING... BLACK BOLT!

HULK KILL!!

NOTHING CAN STOP HULK FROM GETTING *REVENGE!*

37

BUT, AS THE RAGING BEHEMOTH LOOKS FOR **MORE** OF THOSE WHO BETRAYED HIM...

VENGEANCE SHALL NOT BE YOURS...AT SO GREAT A COST AS THE DESTRUCTION OF OUR **REFUGE!**

SWAAACK!

HORSE-MAN DARES TO **CHALLENGE** HULK! THAT WILL BE HIS **LAST** CHALLENGE!

NOT SO, BRUTISH ONE! THOUGH STALLIOR HAS BEEN WRONG IN HIS DEEDS...I STILL HAVE A CHANCE TO ACCOMPLISH ONE **FINAL ACT OF BRAVERY** IN THE NAME OF MY PEOPLE!

§ UUUNNHH! § CHAIN WRAPPED TIGHT AROUND HULK'S BODY... AND HORSE-MAN **PULLING** ON IT!

CAUGHT HULK **OFF-BALANCE!** NOW HULK CAN'T **BREAK FREE!**

I SHOULD NEVER HAVE JOINED MY ACCOMPLICES IN THE **FIRST PLACE**...AND I SHOULD NEVER HAVE FOUGHT BESIDE THEM AGAIN...

...BUT IF, BY DEFEATING YOU, I CAN DO SOME SERVICE FOR THOSE TO WHOM MY **TRUE LOYALTY** LIES...

...THEN I WILL **DIE** ATTEMPTING TO **DO** IT!

AND NOW, IN THE NAME OF BLACK BOLT, WILL I DRAG YOU THROUGH THE STREETS UNTIL YOUR **DEATH**...

...OR AT LEAST UNTIL YOU NO LONGER ARE A THREAT TO OUR **CITY!**

STALLIOR TURNS **AGAINST** US ONCE MORE...BUT HE HAS THE HULK AT HIS **MERCY!**

FIGHT THE BEASTS AGAIN IF YOU **WILL!** BUT IT IS CERTAIN TO BRING DEATH TO YOU--MUCH SOONER THAN THAT WHICH IS ALREADY **INEVITABLE!**

YES...BUT PERHAPS WE CAN TURN HIS TRIUMPH TO OUR ADVANTAGE **ALSO!** LET US **ALL** ATTACK THE GREEN ONE NOW... IN HOPE OF WINNING **PARDON!**

38

QUICKLY! THE CENTAUR HAS THE UPPER HAND... AND WE MUST TAKE *ADVANTAGE* OF IT!

RIGHT! IF WE ATTACK NOW... PERHAPS WE CAN SOMEHOW *DEFEAT* THE HULK!

HURRY, COMRADES! IT WILL TAKE ALL OF OUR *COMBINED STRENGTH* TO BRING THE VICTORY!

¿UUNNHHH!¿

THEN LET LEONUS STRIKE *FIRST!*

IF THE HULK *FALLS* TO US ...THE PEOPLE MIGHT YET *TURN* ON BLACK BOLT...

...AND HAND THE THRONE TO *US* AS THEIR GREATEST HEROES!

SMASH!

THE ENEMY IS *DOWN!* NOW WE MUST KEEP THE *PRESSURE* ON HIM...AND PUMMEL HIM INTO TOTAL *SUBMISSION!*

WE MUST STAY EVER ON THE *OFFENSIVE* ... UNTIL THE BATTLE IS *WON!*

BUT...

YOU STILL DON'T UNDER-STAND THAT *NO ONE* CAN BEAT HULK!

NO ONE!

RAAKK!

NOW IT'S THE *HULK'S* TURN TO FIGHT!

HE'S BROKEN *FREE!* THERE'LL BE NO *STOPPING* HIM NOW!

39

FOR ALL MY JUNGLE-SPAWNED POWER, HE TOSSES ME ABOUT LIKE A MERE *MANNEQUIN!*

YEEAAAA!

NO! WE CANNOT GIVE UP SO *EASILY!* WE MUST BATTLE ON...TO THE VERY *END!*

THEY AREN'T DAMAGING ANY *PROPERTY...*SO BLACK BOLT HAS ORDERED THAT WE LET THEM *DESTROY* EACH OTHER!

ONCE HULK WOULD HAVE LET YOU *LIVE...*

...BUT YOU *BETRAYED* HULK!

AND NOW, HULK WILL SMASH YOU *ALL!*

WHRAAM!

TREE-MAN WILL MAKE GOOD WEAPON TO FINISH *HORSE-MAN!*

NO HOPE REMAINS FOR US! EVEN IF WE *SURVIVE* THE HULK'S ONSLAUGHT... BLACK BOLT WILL SURELY HAVE US *EXECUTED* UNLESS...

...MY *BIRDS OF PREY* CAN YET PRESERVE VICTORY FOR OUR CAUSE!

THEY ARE OUR ONLY CHANCE TO ESCAPE! *TO ME,* MY PETS! FALCONA *SUMMONS* YOU!

40

BUT, WHILE THE UNSUSPECTING HULK FACES YET *ANOTHER* DEADLY CHALLENGE...

AGAIN BLACK BOLT HAS FOILED ME... BECAUSE I MADE THE MISTAKE OF CHOOSING *TREACHEROUS ALLIES!*

HAD I ACTED *ALONE,* AT THIS VERY MOMENT, THE THRONE WOULD BE *MINE!*

INSTEAD, MY WRIST RAY IS GONE ...AND BLACK BOLT DRAGS ME TOWARD MY *LABORATORY...* WHERE HE WILL DOUBTLESSLY ATTEMPT TO DESTROY THE *SOURCE* OF THE RAY'S POWER... THE SUBSTANCE OF *ROMNAR!*

AND HE IS SO *ANGRY,* SO INTENT UPON *ACHIEVING* THAT GOAL ...THERE IS NO WAY I CAN *HALT* HIM!

HOWEVER, SO CRUSHED BY HIS *DEFEAT* IS MAXIMUS, THAT HE FAILS TO SENSE THAT HE IS BEING *FOLLOWED...*

WHILE THE OTHER FOOLS HOPELESSLY BATTLE THE HULK, *NEBULO* WILL YET WREST VICTORY FROM THE JAWS OF *DEFEAT!*

IF ONLY BLACK BOLT'S ANGER REMAINS SO ALL-CONSUMING THAT HE FAILS TO NOTICE MY PRESENCE UNTIL IT IS *TOO LATE!*

THEN, FIVE MINUTES LATER, *INSIDE* THE FORBIDDEN LABORATORY...

I...I AM *SORRY,* MY BROTHER! YOU MUST *FORGIVE* MY ACTS ...AND REMEMBER MY *MENTAL CONDITION!*

THERE IS NO USE! HE WILL NOT BE *DECEIVED* BY ME AGAIN!

PERFECT! BLACK BOLT HAS LEFT THE WRIST RAY *UNGUARDED!*

BLACK BOLT! I *BEG* OF YOU! DO NOT DESTROY THE *SUBSTANCE!* THINK OF THE *POWER* IT WOULD GIVE YOU...IF YOU CAN LEARN TO *CONTROL* IT!

I *HAVE* IT! NOW I NEED ONLY GAIN THE TIME TO *UTILIZE* IT...

AT THAT PRECISE INSTANT...

THE WRIST RAY... IT IS *GONE!*

IF SOMEONE CAN *USE* IT... IT COULD RELEASE THE *SUBSTANCE* ...AND DOOM THE ENTIRE *WORLD!*

42

THEN, AS BLACK BOLT STRUGGLES TO RECOVER FROM SHEER SHOCK...

THERE! THE POWER BELT IS AROUND MY WAIST...AND THE RAY IS READY TO OPERATE!

NOW I NEED ONLY REACH MY COMRADES...AND THE HULK, BEFORE BLACK BOLT CAN ACT!

AND, SPEAKING OF HULKY...

SKREEE!

SKRAAAK!

BIRDS...ATTACK FROM EVERYWHERE! BURYING HULK...SO MANY...CAN'T FIGHT THEM ALL OFF!

HOWEVER, THE HULK WON'T NEED TO DEFEAT THE BIRDS PHYSICALLY, FOR, AT THAT MOMENT...BLACK BOLT IN HIS FRANTIC SEARCH FOR THE WRIST RAY SEES MILLIONS OF BIRDS...IN THE TRIAL ARENA! HE REALIZES IT CAN ONLY BE THE DOING OF FALCONA!

THROUGH CONTROL OF THE VERY ATMOSPHERE, BLACK BOLT SHATTERS HER POWER OVER THE CREATURES...

THE...AIR... SUDDENLY...VERY THIN! I...CAN HARDLY...BREATHE!

43

AND, WITHIN A FEW SECONDS, THE CARNIVOROUS BIRDS FLY CRAZILY INTO THE DISTANCE... DESPERATELY IN SEARCH OF A LUNGFULL OF PRECIOUS *AIR!* THEN...

WE CAN *BREATHE* AGAIN! YOU ONLY REMOVED THE AIR FROM OUR ATMOSPHERE LONG ENOUGH TO PANIC THE *BIRDS*... AND MAKE THEM *FLEE!*

BUT NOW, YOU HAVE LEFT IN THEIR WAKE A FAR *GREATER* MENACE... THE *GREEN-SKINNED GIANT!*

BIRDS ARE *GONE*... BUT MEN STILL STAND TO *CHALLENGE* HULK!

BUT, LET THEM *COME!* HULK WILL BEAT *ALL* OF THEM!

SEE, BLACK BOLT? HE'S *BERSERK*... THINKING ONLY OF CRUSHING EVERYTHING THAT STANDS IN HIS *PATH!*

EVER SINCE HULK WAS *BROUGHT* HERE... MEN HAVE TRIED TO *USE* HIM ... AND *DESTROY* HIM!

NOW HULK HAS HAD *ENOUGH!* SO, EITHER *ATTACK* ME... OR HULK WILL ATTACK *YOU!*

THEN, BEFORE BLACK BOLT CAN SIZE UP THE SITUATION...

YOU'VE WAITED *TOO LONG!*

NOW HULK WILL *FIGHT* YOU... TO THE *FINISH!*

44

THE GIANT DARES TO *STRIKE* BLACK BOLT!

NOW SURELY OUR LEADER WILL SEE THAT HE IS *EVIL*... AND HE WILL SMITE THE INTRUDER *DOWN!*

DO NOT BE TOO *CERTAIN!* LOOK...THE CREATURE ADVANCES ON BLACK BOLT *AGAIN!*

HULK HIT YOU ONCE... AND YOU'RE STILL *STANDING*...

...BUT *NO ONE* STANDS AFTER HULK SMASHES HIM A *SECOND TIME!*

BUT, AS THE RAGING GREEN GOLIATH MOVES IN FOR THE *KILL*...

KERWHACKKK!

≷UNNHHH!⟨

45

THEN, BEFORE THE STUNNED HULK CAN CLAMBER TO HIS *FEET*... BLACK BOLT STRIKES HIM ONCE MORE WITH A DEADLY *ELECTRON BLAST*...

ZZZAAATTT!

AAGGGHHH!

HOWEVER, IN SPITE OF THE INCOMPARABLE FORCES UTILIZED *AGAINST* HIM... THE HULK KNOWS NOT THE MEANING OF *DEFEAT*...

...AND THE PILE-DRIVING BLOW OF HIS GARGANTUAN FIST TO THE GROUND SENDS THE INHUMAN MONARCH TUMBLING TO THE *GROUND*...

YOU'RE LIKE ALL THE *OTHERS*! THINK ONLY OF *KILLING* HULK! NEVER TRY TO *UNDERSTAND*!

BUT YOU'RE THEIR *LEADER*... AND IF HULK BEATS *YOU*... THEN MAYBE OTHERS WILL LEAVE ME *ALONE*!

PUNY RAYS CAN'T HURT HULK IF THEY CAN'T *HIT* HIM! AND HULK WON'T GIVE YOU A CHANCE TO *USE* THEM AGAIN!

...YOU ARE *STRONG*...BUT NOT STRONG ENOUGH TO BEAT HULK *HAND-TO-HAND*! NOW YOU CAN *GIVE UP*...OR HULK WILL CRUSH YOU WITH HIS *BARE HANDS*!

46

BUT, AS THE SHEER, BRUTE STRENGTH OF THE HULK IS ABOUT TO CRUSH THE VERY *LIFE* FROM BLACK BOLT'S BODY... THE MOST POWERFUL OF ALL IN-HUMANS DESPERATELY RESORTS TO THE MOST DEADLY POWER OF *ALL*... HE OPENS HIS MOUTH, AND *WHISPERS ONE WORD*... CAUSING A WAVE OF *SONIC SOUND*...

PRAYING ALL THE WHILE THAT THE GREAT, MUSCLE-LADEN TISSUES OF THE HULK'S BODY WILL ABSORB THE *BRUNT* OF THE SONIC BOLT'S DESTRUCTIVE POWERS--!

THEN, AS THE VIBRATIONS WHICH HAVE SHAKEN THE VERY *FOUNDATIONS* OF THE GREAT REFUGE GRADUALLY SUBSIDE... BLACK BOLT SEES THAT HIS GAMBLE HAS *PAID OFF!* THE DEVASTATING BOLT WAS ENOUGH TO *FREE* HIM OF THE HULK...*

*IF YOU THINK THAT *CRATER* IS SOMETHING, JUST REMEMBER WHAT HAPPENED ONCE WHEN BLACK BOLT *SHOUTED*--OR ELSE LOOK IT UP IN *F.F. #57!*

47

As BLACK BOLT moves to stand over the still, almost *LIFELESS* form of his fallen adversary ...HIS attention is suddenly diverted by a grim, deadly challenge from *BEHIND*...

SURRENDER YOUR *THRONE*, BLACK BOLT...OR BE HELD FOREVER RESPONSIBLE FOR THE WORLD'S *DESTRUCTION!*

MAKE YOUR DECISION *QUICKLY*... FOR EVEN NOW I BEGIN TO UNLEASH THE VERY POWER WHICH CAN SPELL THE END FOR US *ALL!*

INVISIBLE MAN... WHO PRETENDED TO BE HULK'S FRIEND... THREATENING TO *KILL* EVERYONE!

HULK TIRED... MUSCLES ACHING ...BUT MUST *STOP* SHADOW MAN!

GET OUT OF THE WAY! THIS IS HULK'S FIGHT!

STOP! YOU WITLESS FOOL! I'M YOUR *FRIEND!* YOU DON'T WANT TO FIGHT *ME!*

SHADOW-MAN *LIES!* YOU ONLY *USED* HULK ...AND NOW HULK WILL *PUNISH* YOU FOR IT!

KERRAACCKK!

YOU'VE MADE A FOOL OF HULK FOR THE *LAST* TIME!

48

THEN, AS NEBULO COLLAPSES FROM THE FORCE OF THE HULK'S *BLOW...*

NEBULO HAS *FALLEN...* AND BLACK BOLT LEAPS FOR THE *WEAPON!*

¡UUNNHH! WEAPON'S RAYS AGAIN STRIKE...

QUICKLY... MOVE IN TO *ARREST* NEBULO!

BEFORE THE WRATH OF THE HULK CAN ONCE AGAIN BE *AROUSED...*

YOU GIVE HULK HAND... TO HELP HIM *UP!*

HULK DOESN'T *UNDERSTAND!* FIRST YOU *FIGHT* HULK... THEN YOU *HELP* HIM!

WHY DO YOU *ASSIST* THE CREATURE, BLACK BOLT? HE NEARLY DESTROYED THE *REFUGE!*

HE SHOULD BE *EXECUTED* BEFORE HE CAN RUN WILD AMONG US *AGAIN!*

BUT, BLACK BOLT SIGNIFIED HIS ANSWER IS *NO!*

BLACK BOLT DECREES THAT THE GREEN ONE BE *SPARED...* JUST AS HE HAS SPARED US ALL FROM THE TYRANNY OF *NEBULO!*

BUT, HE WASN'T TRYING TO SAVE *US!* HE ONLY SOUGHT REVENGE ON *NEBULO!* GORGON MAINTAINS THAT HE SHOULD BE *DESTROYED!*

PEOPLE *STILL* HATE HULK... SO HULK'S FIGHT STILL ISN'T *FINISHED!*

BUT, AS THE HULK'S BLOOD ONCE MORE BEGINS TO *BOIL*--AND AS BLACK BOLT ATTEMPTS TO SHOW HIM THAT HE MEANS NO FURTHER *HARM...*

49

BLACK BOLT IS MY RULER...BUT HIS HEART IS TOO *SOFT!* IS THERE NO WAY I CAN MAKE HIM SEE THE DEADLY *MENACE* THIS MONSTER PRESENTS TO US!

BRUJUNH.

AND, IN BITTER FRUSTRATION GORGON STAMPS HIS FOOT ON THE GROUND...SETTING OFF A TREMOR WHICH KNOCKS BOTH THE HULK AND BLACK BOLT OFF THEIR *FEET*...

BUT, AS THE HULK STORMS TOWARD GORGON...

WAIT! BLACK BOLT WISHES YOU TO UNDERSTAND THAT WAS NOT OF HIS *DOING!*

HE BIDS THE HULK *LISTEN* TO HIM...FOR BLACK BOLT *DOES* UNDERSTAND!

BLACK BOLT REALIZES THAT THE HULK HAS SPENT A LIFETIME OF *RECLUSE*...

...BUT NOW HE OFFERS YOU SOME- THING BETTER... *FRIENDSHIP*...AND *REFUGE*...HERE, AMONG *US!*

NO!

MAYBE *BLACK BOLT* UNDER- STANDS...BUT OTHER PEOPLE DON'T! THEY STILL *FEAR* HULK...

...SO, NO MATTER *WHAT* BLACK BOLT SAYS, HULK COULD NEVER *LIVE* HERE IN PEACE!

THEN, AT LEAST *LEAVE* HERE IN PEACE... AND KNOW THAT BLACK BOLT SHALL BE FOREVER *INDEBTED* TO YOU!

AND NOW, BLACK BOLT BIDS YOU *FAREWELL*... AND *GODSPEED!*

50

FINALLY, MINUTES LATER, A LONELY, BROODING FIGURE STANDS IN THE MOUNTAINS HIGH ABOVE THE GREAT REFUGE... AND TURNS FOR A FINAL, LONGING LOOK AT THE ONE PLACE HE MIGHT HAVE CALLED... *HOME!*

HULK COULD HAVE STAYED THERE! BLACK BOLT MIGHT HAVE BEEN A REAL *FRIEND...*

...BUT IT WOULDN'T HAVE *HELPED*...BECAUSE EVERYONE ELSE *HATED* ME!

MAYBE SOMEDAY, HULK WILL FIND WHOLE *CITY* FULL OF MEN LIKE BLACK BOLT!

BUT, UNTIL THEN, HULK CAN ONLY *RUN*...AND *HIDE*...AND *HATE!*

THE END